THE COMPLETE
TRAILER PARK BOYS

How to enjoy the Trailer Park Boys when your cable is out!

THE OFFICIAL SUNNYVALE FAN GUIDE

MATTHEW SiBiGA and DON WININGER

RANDOM HOUSE CANADA

www.randomhouse.ca

Library and Archives Canada Cataloguing in Publication

Sibiga, Matthew
    The complete Trailer Park Boys : how to enjoy the Trailer Park Boys
when your cable is out / Matthew Sibiga & Don Wininger.

ISBN 978-0-307-35581-2

    1. Trailer park boys (Television program).   I. Wininger, Don   II. Title.

PN1992.77.T73S52 2007   791.45'72   C2006-905701-X

All photos appear courtesy of TPB Productions

Text and Jacket Design: Don Wininger

Printed and bound in the United States of America

10 9 8 7 6 5 4 3 2 1

Cory and Trevor were not harmed during the production of this book.

Produced with the participation of the

Canadian Television Fund

created by the Government of Canada
and the Canadian Cable Industry

Telefilm Canada: Equity Investment Program
CTF: Licence Fee Program

To the pursuit of simple pleasures

Introduction

We have to be honest. We asked two Governors General —one past and one present—to write the introduction to *The Complete Trailer Park Boys*, thinking it would be an honour to introduce the most important cultural document produced this year in Canada. To our dismay, the first symbolic head of state we approached—Michaëlle Jean, Canada's new (and kind of hot) Governor General—told us to "frig off." Well, that's not really true. (And while we're being so truthful, we didn't really speak to Madame Jean —the reply was conveyed via a short email from a temp allegedly working in Her Excellency's office.)

Dejected but not defeated, we contacted the office of previous Governor General, Adrienne Clarkson, and before we could even tell the assistant who answered the phone that Madame Clarkson wasn't really our first choice to write the introduction—but would she do it anyway?—the obnoxious lackey also told us to "frig off!"

(Again, while we're being honest, Adrienne Clarkson only came to mind because she was the only other Governor General we could think of, and we really wanted to get some sort of Governor General to write this damned introduction.) Fresh out of options, we were feeling as unloved as Cory and Trevor during a heist. However, we still needed some sort of "intelligent" name to lend intellectual heft to this book.

We consulted Captain Morgan for inspiration and wouldn't you know it, we actually thought of an author. Remember Franklin W. Dixon, the guy who wrote all the Hardy Boys books? He's a writer and he's reputed to be Canadian . . . but he's also reputed to be dead. Fortunately we arrived at a more workable solution before getting totally desperate and hitting the Jiffy Wine. Why not us? *We* wrote the book, so would we consider writing the introduction? I asked Don and he agreed at once to my request.

—Matthew Sibiga

About three years ago I was channel surfing and came across a man with overly stylish hair wearing track pants and a checked shirt. He was wrestling a shirtless man with a large stomach and tight white trousers. They were kicking up plenty of dust and firing expletives at each other while being filmed by a hand-held camera. It appeared to be a spoof on the popular show *Cops*. A few months later I was flipping channels again when I caught the opening theme song of this same show. The lilting piano and sepia scenes of children at play transported me back to a gentler time, reminiscent of Mayberry, Andy Taylor and Aunt Bea. The serenity was soon broken, however, not by the soft spoken Sherrif Taylor, but by a pee-stained park supervisor named Mr. Lahey and that shirtless guy, this time dressed as a bumblebee, who announces to the park that he and Mr. Lahey are gay. Not sure that Barney Fife had the same relationship with his boss, but I was hooked.

Just like the folksy, lovable characters of early-sixties television, the residents of Sunnyvale were just looking to get by in their own small world, with the help of a little booze, dope, petty crime and mastery of four-letter words. Ricky, Julian, Bubbles and the gang might be rough on each other, and the occasional musical celebrity, but their chaos has way more bark than bite. Friendship truly matters to them, along with finding pleasures in simple things like pepperoni and pickled eggs. Surely, the show's messages ring true, not just in Sunnyvale or Mayberry, but in any community that likes to BBQ and throw the occasional bottle.

Shortly after a randomly selected publisher agreed to do our *Trailer Park Boys* book, Matt and I flew to Halifax to meet Barrie Dunn and Michael Volpe—two of the show's three producers—Karen Wentzell completes the trio. We talked about favourite scenes and why the show has become so popular across Canada. Our hope was that our creative efforts would reflect theirs, along with the tremendous talents of director Mike Clattenburg. We met Mike on the set the next day and he cast us as Sunnyvale police extras in that day's shoot. It was quite a thrill, even if we didn't have speaking parts, just eating parts (doughnuts). Several times during filming I saw Mike try unsuccessfully to contain his laughter. It was a pleasant reminder how free of pretense *Trailer Park Boys* is and how genuine its humour remains. It's a well-written, hilarious show with terrific actors, producers and director who really enjoy themselves. It's very Canadian that way, and I think the boys have woven themselves a permanent place in our country's cultural fabric.

If you enjoy this book, even in small measure, as much as you have enjoyed *Trailer Park Boys*' first six seasons, well we think that's fucking decent! For those whose book learnin' could be gooder, we've included lots of photos.

—Don Wininger

CONTENTS

Photographs by Mike Tompkins and Scott Munn

Fans of the *Trailer Park Boys* would agree that the setting of Sunnyvale and its characters are visually unique. Co-writer Matthew and I met Mike Tompkins while visiting the set during shooting of a season-seven episode. He was kind enough to take the above shot of us with the boys, fresh from our acting debuts as cops. We are particularly grateful to Mike for his wonderful photos that are featured throughout this book. He has a definite talent for capturing the humour of the show with a single still. He began shooting the *Trailer Park Boys* midway through season two, and his work represents the majority of photos used in this book. When we received copies of his work, it was as much fun as Bubbles unwrapping his bubble-maker. Also included are some great shots from Scott Munn who captured the show in season one and into the year two. We thank both of you for these very enjoyable photographs.

—Don Wininger

THE CHARACTERS

"Fuckin' best trailer park in the goddamn world, right here."

"Knock, knock."

Ricky looking tough while riding his hog... more like a piglet actually.

Education

"We're getting real close to going on this cruise, but the problem is tomorrow is the deadline for the down payment of the tickets and we have to have three thousand dollars to put down or we are going to lose our tickets. But it just so happens that Trinity's school just had this fundraiser at school to go on a class trip and we raised three fuckin' grand in the trailer park alone [if you're counting, that's about 30,000 beer bottles]. And basically what happens is Trinity is not allowed to go on the trip now she got caught smoking on school grounds, which is bullshit. What we said was 'fuck that,' we're going to go down there and take the bottles back 'cause they're ours anyway and put them towards our own fuckin' trip. It just pisses me off; the problem with school and education system complicate everything up for me and it's just bullshit. Fuck the education system! We're doing it our own fuckin' way."

"Maybe people think I'm stupid; I know I'm not stupid. I've taken about seven or eight courses in jail in my three times. I've graduated from all the courses, except for two of them."

"It's not that I'm not a big fan of school, I guess it's just that . . . you know . . . what is school? What does it do for ya? I guess people say you learn stuff there and that. I did okay there, I guess, until I wasn't allowed back. It's overrated. Back in history you couldn't go to school, you just had to kinda learn it on your own. That's what I do, I just learn things . . . I watch Julian or other people and you just learn how to do your own stuff. You don't need people there at the front of the class telling you what to do and what not to do. I don't even know what the whole deal of school is. Who came up with that idea? There's a better way to do it, that's all."

"Treena's all gung-ho about me getting my grade ten and I don't want to let her down. And to be honest, I kinda wouldn't mind getting my grad ten anyways, 'cause then I could talk to people better. And then maybe I'll understand what people are saying all the time, 'cause right now I don't."

The Importance of Children's Birthdays

"I haven't seen Lucy and Trinity since, I think it was her seventh birthday—no, it was her eighth birthday, that's right, it was her eighth birthday. But I bought her a cake that said 'Happy Seventh Birthday.' It was just one of those mistakes anyone could make. It's no big deal. The point is, I did buy her a birthday cake."

Ecology

"I've noticed if you throw something into a body of water like a lake or ocean, and you come back the next day, it's gone. Somehow it takes it away and filters it through like a garbage compactor. It's not really littering if you ask me."

Intelligence

"If you're not smart, as long as you've got someone smart around you that is smart, you're smart too."

5

Ricky
ON SOMETHING

His Intelligence Versus Julian's

"I don't know who's telling you that Julian's the brains of this operation, but, I mean, we're both the brains of the operation. He's smart, I'm smart. We're smart in different ways, I guess. I mean, I'm smart by playing hockey—doing things like growing dope and that. He's smarter when it comes to clear thinking, explaining things to people. That's why we are a good team, because I'm good at the hands-on and applicatory stuff and he explains things in a clear kinda way. When he thinks . . . when he talks . . . for fuck's sakes! I'm havin' trouble talkin', but I am smart!"

The Importance of Being a Role Model

"I like to be a role model for Treena and the other kids in the park. I think it is good. If I had a role model when I was younger—learning how to grow dope—things would have been a lot smoother, 'cause now if some kid wants to grow dope they can talk to me. Instead of growing dope through denial and error, they're going to get it right the first time and have some good dope."

Ricky on the Magic of Books

"Books make it so much easier to understand really hard thinking and stuff. They make it a lot clearer."

The Art of the Unintelligible Apology

"Bubbles, I know we sometimes get a little caught up in this Freedom 35 stuff and get mixed up and you go home thinking about stuff and thinking about what your friends were thinking and things get all scrambled up like a big pan of eggs. You know what I mean?"

Ricky Aiming for the Moon and Beyond!

"I got my grade ten! I got fifty-seven percent, which is the best mark I ever got without cheating, so I'm really happy. I can't quite believe it still. I never thought I was going to get my grade ten—ever in my whole life. Maybe now I can get my grade eleven. Who knows!"

Cory and Trevor's Intelligence

"I know they are stupid as fuck but they are getting a lot more smartable."

Smooth Punchline Delivery

"Hey Lahey, knock, knock."—Ricky
"Who's there?"—Lahey
"Mr. Stupidy Head is fucking pissing me off right now, thinks he's captain of the shitliner, and by the way, your fish sticks suck, so fuck off and open the gate!"—Ricky

Living in a Car

"People's first impression of me, that I'm livin' in a car, is that it's not that great. Really, it's not that bad. Look at me, I mean, I can cook every meal I need to and growing dope in the back seat, which is pretty good."

Tricking Cops

"Cops? I dunno, it's like a board game that you're good at, I guess. Some people are good at different board games and that's the board game I'm good at."

The Insurance Business

"The guy is a fuckin' dick [the jewellery store owner they are about to rob]. I sold him a bunch of weed he never paid me for, so fuck him. I mean, that's what insurance companies are for. It's no big deal, he's going to get his money back."

The Importance of a Wedding Ring

"The thing is, when you are shopping for a ring, you have to take your time, because it is my wife we're talkin' about. She's not going to be wearing one of those cubic zarcabion fuckin' things. She's got to have a nice ring."

Drankin' and Drovin'

"There are certain accidents that you may be drunk and on drugs, but it is going to happen anyway whether you are or not."

Absence Makes the Heart Grow Fonder

"Taking a break from dope is even a good thing because when you smoke dope again, you get a lot more fucked up."

Making the Best of a Bad Situation

"I'm glad I went to jail and the only thing I really miss is having regular dope all the time, getting drunk regularly—and I miss Lucy and Trinity. Other than that, I fuckin' love being in jail."

The Economics of Weed

"This is going to be the best idea I ever had. I mean, think about it, dope goes for a way more awesomer price in jail. I mean, it's supply and command. If you're in jail, you're lucky if you get stoned once a week and when you do, the dope sucks. I don't see anything wrong with having dope in jail and there's going to be dope in jail; we may as well be the ones supplying it."

Ricky
ON SOMETHING

Ricky
ON SOMETHING

Responsibility

"Anyway, I got smokin' beat. Quit that. Quit drinkin', [school's] going to be easy. I'm trying to set some hard goals for myself. Thinking a lot about maybe going back to school. That's the sort of stuff I think Lucy wants to see and it helps little Trinity get things going on in her head 'cause she saw me do them and that helps for her to help with her thinkin'. I dunno, think it's time for me to grow up and be a responsible man. I think I'm there."

Justice for All

"Look, I can't speak without swearing and I've only got my grade ten. I haven't had a cigarette since I've been arrested and I'm ready to fuckin' snap—so I'd like to make a request under make the People's Choices and Voices Act, that I can smoke and swear in your courtroom 'cause if I can't smoke and swear—I'm fucked. And so are all of these guys. I won't be able to properly express myself at a court level and that's bullshit. It's not fair and if you ask me, I think it's a fuckin' mistrial."

Self-Preservation

"Shoot yourself, don't shoot me."

Keeping the Humour Short and Sweet

"Knock, knock"—Ricky
"Who's there?"—Sam Losco
"Fuck off!"

Why He'll Never Study Psychiatry in Vienna

"Over the last couple of weeks—I don't know what's going with Lahey, but he is starting to lose it. He's drinking a lot more—today especially, he's fuckin' drunk and he is starting to lose it. He's starting to push my buttons and that's not cool and I'm not going to allow that to happen. It's like he's got these things going on upstairs in his brain compartment that aren't working properly. He's got this pikeological shit going on and I tell ya, he better watch himself. He's going to get hammered—big time."

Nepotism

"Knock, knock"—Ricky
"Who's there?"—Lahey
"Somebody"
"Sombody who?
"Somebody whose ex-wife owns the trailer park is the only reason he got a fuckin' job as a trailer park supervisor got fired from the police force because he fucked up big time but we're not going to talk about that one are we?"

Nothing like a good smoke after burning down your dad's trailer.

Car Livin' Is the Life for Me

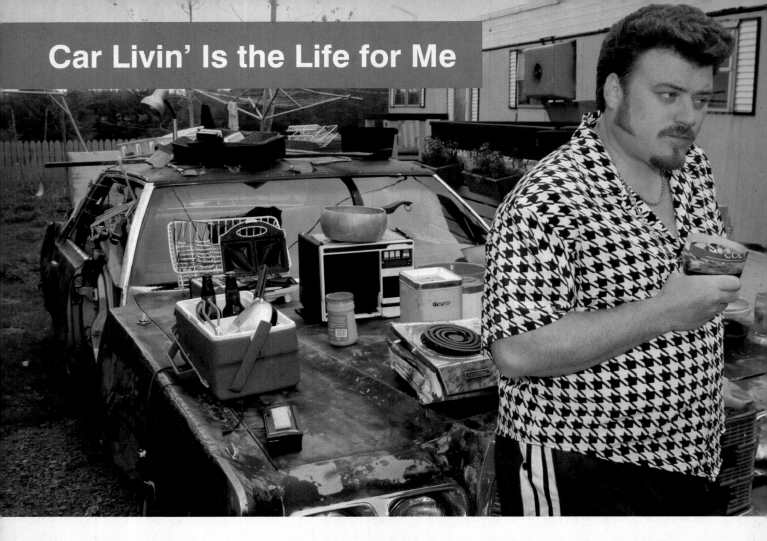

"Livin' in my car is fuckin' awesome," says Ricky as he checks the readiness of the chicken fingers toasting in his rooftop toaster oven. Now we're not talking about some exotic outdoor kitchen atop a swanky condo. No, Ricky's kitchen is an old toaster oven that sits on the roof of his car, and it cooks some of the tastiest chicken fingers this side of Chicoutimi. The toaster oven is just one of the many features of Ricky's home—known by some as the Shitmobile.

If it were Hollywood, his address would be 77 Shitmobile Strip, but at Sunnyvale it's simply Ricky's car parked in the yard next to Julian's trailer. Before becoming Ricky's home, the car was just a 1975 New Yorker given to him by Julian. "It's not every day your friend, or anybody for that matter, gives you a home," recalls Ricky. "That's pretty fuckin' cool." Quite a car when new to the market, the New Yorker came fully loaded from the factory. Its transition from car to home brought with it plenty of amenities for the owner. Ricky proudly gave us a tour.

First stop, the back seat/bedroom. "It's fucking huge back there," says Ricky. This back seat is built for action, and, of course, those long, lazy weekends when one wakes to the midday sun. Spring-action seats give plenty of support and comfort plus really hold up well when things get heavy. The big bench is upholstered in green synthetic cloth, as are the matching headliner and the armrests, which double as pillow supports or quaint ottomans. Shades of emerald add a luxurious hint. Bedside ashtrays are integrated into the armrests.

The front-seat family room features an entertainment centre complete with AM radio and under-dash eight-track player. The large dashboard is about coffee-table

size and will accommodate a full take-out chicken spread when entertaining indoors. "That front seat's as comfortable as one of the lazy-fucker chairs," says Ricky. "I can drive home and pass out right behind the wheel, and because it's my home I don't have to get outta my car and pass out in the street or a garden or something like that. It's fucking great, and safer, I guess." Open windows on both side doors facilitate a refreshing breeze. "These stay open pretty much all the time," Ricky tells us. The kitchen range rests conveniently beneath his home's immense hood. "This engine does it all, way better than some shitty home. You need a furnace, power lines, stove in a house. They sell all these things separately and fuck the guy in the house. In my car, this engine does it all and I can drive my house to the LC or to get some chips, pepperoni, whatever the fuck I need. I've never seen an engine that can just move a house down the road. Who drives their house to the store for chips?"

No Plumbing? No Problem.

Entertaining is a breeze.
Let's take this party indoors.

When he's finished some good cooking on the engine, Ricky demonstrates how the hood closes to become an outdoor patio table. "I can put about a thousand or a hundred or even more drinks on this. In the morning I clean it up in about . . ."—Ricky reaches for the clearing stick, and sweeps it across the hood—"three seconds." The Shitmobile also features outdoor running water, thanks to a neighbour's hose taped to the side of Ricky's roof, and free cable, conveniently supplied by wires running into nearby trailers. "If they ran the wires on the inside, they wouldn't want you to have cable, would they? It's like a water fountain. They wouldn't leave them in plain sight if they didn't want you to have a drink or even *Littlest Hobo* reruns."

A humongous trunk provides abundant closet space and can hold empties, dope, cash, guns, wheelchairs and Cory and Trevor—all at the same time. The laundry room is located on the outside of the car, which is great because you don't want to track dirt into the car. And clothes dried outside on a line have that sunny, spring-fresh smell. There's something to be said for car living: freedom, simplicity, flexibility—and if you don't like your neighbours, simply turn the key. "Would I like to live in a nice trailer? Sure, who wouldn't? But fuck it, this is my home, and when the dogs aren't barking, it's a good life. At least I don't have to live in one of those little bug cars or a Pekingese import."

We agree, Ricky. Car living's pretty fuckin' awesome.

REPORT CARD

English: Miss [redacted]

Richard has made a concerted effort this term to improve his reading skills. I think we might see greater improvement were he to spend an occasional evening reading a book instead of getting drunk with his friends. Richard's verbal skills are certainly colourful and he has a fine command of expletives, although they do cloud his ability to complete sentences with any semblance of grammatical structure. His study of Shakespeare's Taming of the Shrew was a particular challenge, as it is for most young minds. However, Richard's suggestion that fair Kate might be calmed with rum and hashish was certainly inappropriate. Richard struggled on many of the formal tests, but achieved a passing grade thanks to his enthusiasm in class. Well done, Richard.

Math: Mr. [redacted]

Had it not been for Ricky's keen abilities and high marks in the weights and measures studied this term, he might have failed to achieve a passing grade. Strangely, he breezed through the section on grams and kilograms, yet hadn't the slightest idea of how to convert metres to kilometres.

Science: Mr. [redacted]

Ricky is a gifted student who should consider a career in botany. Quite frankly, his skills in grafting plants and developing rapid-growth methods amaze us all. We strongly recommend he apply for a scholarship at the Atlantic Horticultural Institute.

Chemistry: Mr. [redacted]

Rarely does a student show so much interest in chemicals. Our studies on carbon compounds and alcohols were almost too fascinating for Ricky. He wanted to see, smell and taste all the compounds. So daring, but potentially dangerous, I'm afraid. His lab work was inspired, except he had to be warned repeatedly not to light cigarettes on his Bunsen burner.

Physical Education: Mr. [redacted]

Ricky was a dominant athlete this year, thanks to his generous size. Many of his classmates were less than half his weight. He was untouchable in intramural floor hockey and averaged fourteen goals a game. He set a grade ten rebounding record in basketball and would have easily won the heavyweight wrestling title had he not thrown punches in the championship match. Ricky was below average in health class. He scored poorly on nutrition and failed to complete the timed mile run. But overall, Ricky was the man!

Industrial Arts: Mr. [redacted]

Ricky had the potential for a better grade. His skill at crafting in metal and wood was undermined by the fact that the objects he produced, though functional, were always either illegal or certainly against school policy. The end of term project was especially difficult to complete for all students this year due to an unfortunate disappearance of many of the shop's tools.

Music: Mrs. [redacted]

Ricky struggled to find an appreciation for classical music. His repeated insistence that we play something called "Helix" became tiresome. Ricky missed many classes and when he did attend he often appeared to be suffering from some form of foggy dementia. He shows no signs of having musical talent and was reduced to playing two sticks for percussion, which he brazenly substituted with pepperoni during the class's presentation of the Pirates of Penzance. He could have been a wonderful swashbuckler, but perhaps he's one of the few people in this world who can't find a place in his heart for the love of Gilbert and Sullivan.

Student Average: 57%

JULIAN

"This can't fail, boys."

You Could
WIN
A DREAM
DATE
WITH JULIAN

Your night begins with a ride in a stretch "lemonzine." It's fully stocked with booze. Don't worry about having to pee. The driver will pull over whenever you ask him.

Head to the mall, where Cory and Trevor will fix you up with all the gum you can chew.

Stop by an open field for some target shooting. You'll be amazed how many things can take a bullet.

Let the master himself mix you a drink. You've never had a rum and cola this good before. Guaranteed.

Hang out with Julian and his really cool friends.

Engage in at least ten minutes of deep conversation with Julian. It's almost better than sex.

14

Give This Man a Hand

Perhaps most impressive among Julian's many admirable traits is his ability—and sheer will—to adapt to his disability. He simply refuses to let it effect how much joy he gets out of life. After losing the use of one arm to a glass of rum and cola, he could have sunk into despondency—he did no such thing. Where most people would give in to feelings of anguish, Julian decided to embrace life with all the gusto that he could muster, as if to say to the world, "Never mind that I can only use one arm at any given time, I'm ready for life and whatever it throws at me!" He transcends the limitations that carrying his drink imposes on whichever hand is holding it through the development of remarkable motor skills.

Case in point: have you ever noticed his sense of balance? The man never spills his drink. Ever. Julian has endured a rolling car wreck and emerged with drink and dignity intact. If his left hand is occupied with a gun, his right hand adapts to carry his cool, refreshing drink; if he has a hockey stick in his right hand, his left hand takes over responsibility for that fragile, precious glass. The guy can do more things with one hand than most people can do with two. Why Cirque du Soleil hasn't themed a one-armed show around this big, inspirational bastard in the black T-shirt and shades is beyond us.

To celebrate this man, who epitomizes humanity's will to overcome adversity, we have compiled a comprehensive list of the many things Julian can accomplish one-handed. We hope you find it as inspiring as we do.

- Play road hockey.
- Rob grocery stores.
- Do whatever he does with Officer Erica Miller.
- Pour rum and colas.
- Bootleg vodka.
- Deal with Cyrus.
- Visit Mrs. Peterson, who would rather he had the use of both hands.
- Take care of Sparky the dog (actually, he didn't do this so well . . . forget it).
- Deal with Mr. Lahey (who doesn't hold a drink particularly well with two hands, never mind one).
- Not slap Cory and Trevor's hands.
- Steal Christmas trees.
- Tell Ricky to "Let me do the thinking" (you try that one-handed; it's not easy).
- Conduct spirited shootouts.
- Ignore Lucy.
- Rescue Randy, who's in a bumblebee suit.
- Dodge Bottle Kids attacks.
- Blow Conky's fuckin' head off.
- Seduce Candy.

We salute you, Julian!

JULIAN
AN INSPIRATION TO US ALL

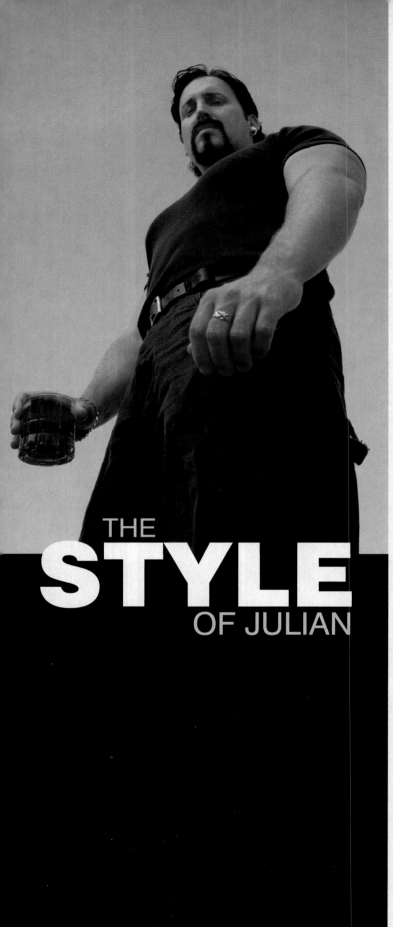

Let's face it, there is virtually nobody in Sunnyvale that *GQ* or *In Style* would ever deem good enough to write about (although rumour has it that *National Geographic* is investigating how Randy's midriff seems to be developing its own gravity and weather systems). At first, second and third glance, the place appears utterly devoid of the pretentious, disposable nonsense that makes the New York and Toronto fashion scenes so forgettable. But upon a fourth glance, astute fashionistas quickly realize what they should have seen on their second or maybe third glance: Julian looks pretty fuckin' sharp!

No shortage of great men have dressed in black: Johnny Cash, the original man in black (God bless 'im); David Hasselhoff's car, KITT, in *Knight Rider*; "Joliet" Jake and Elwood Blues, the Blues Brothers; Tommy Lee Jones and Will Smith in *Men In Black*; D-Day, from the infamous Delta House of *Animal House* fame, was known to put on a black T-shirt from time to time; and Hoss Cartwright of *Bonanza* occasionally wore a black vest. (The Friendly Giant never wore black, only green felt.) All greats, to be sure, but none quite equal Julian's inimitable personal style—except maybe Miles Davis, but even he would be asking Julian where he shopped. And while we're talking about Miles Davis, how about we rename his famous album, *Kind of Blue,* to *Kind of Black?* Or better yet, *Kind of Julian?* Other great music with the black motif? How about AC/DC's classic, hard-rocking album, *Back In Black*; Zeppelin's "Black Dog"; Black Sabbath; Black Forest ham (it's not music, but it's damn good on a marbled rye); Black Power (not music either, but it was a kick-ass social movement); and Spinal Tap's infamous *Smell the Glove* album, which was described as "none more black" by bassist Derek Smalls. If Julian were a football team, he'd be the Oakland Raiders. Notice a pattern? Black is pretty damn stylish and pretty damn cool. If Julian were ever to leave Sunnyvale and find himself on the streets of New York or Toronto, you can bet some astute designer would steal his look and we would be seeing Julian Couture at the next fall show. In honour of the sharpest-dressed man never sung about by ZZ Top, we list here the key ingredients of Julian's incomparable look.

THE
STYLE
OF JULIAN

- Black T-shirt, tight (just ask Mr. Lahey)
- Black belt
- Black trousers, sometimes blue jeans, neither too tight (sorry Mr. Lahey)
- Black shoes
- Black sunglasses, to accent his gold wrist chains, necklace and earrings
- Black drink, mixed with such cool the ice never melts
- Black hair, groomed in perfect balance with facial hair
- Black goatee, trimmed with a Mercedes Benz engineer's attention to detail

JULIAN SPRING COLLECTION

JULIAN SUMMER COLLECTION

JULIAN COUTURE

JULIAN FALL COLLECTION

JULIAN WINTER COLLECTION

"This Can't Fail, Boys"

Julian might be the coolest guy to ever utter these words, but he certainly isn't the first. History is full of actors, inventors, politicians, coaches, producers, soldiers, you name it, who have assured their people that everything is under control, the situation is in hand, it's going to be cool—in short, men who say, This can't fail, boys." Julian is actually in good company when it comes to presiding over plans that go just a little bit off the rails. In fact, next to some of the fiascos listed here, the boys ending up in jail is practically a success.

1. When the designers of the Hindenburg decided to use hydrogen rather than helium to provide the German airship's lift, one engineer was overheard to remark, "This can't fail, boys." Julian would have filled the airship with the fumes of burning hash.

2. Remember when President George W. Bush announced to the world from the deck of the USS Abraham Lincoln that as far as he was concerned, the war in Iraq was mission accomplished? Translation: "This can't fail, boys." Julian would have stayed home and peddled some hash.

3. On four separate Super Bowl Sundays, just before kickoff, Buffalo Bills coach Marv Levy was heard to say to his team, "This can't fail, boys." The only super bowl Julian acknowledges is the one that holds his big chunk of burning hash.

4. In 1915, the First Lord of the Admiralty, who later became the cigar-loving British prime minister, Winston Churchill, commissioned plans to launch an attack on Gallipoli. This is a great example of a "This can't fail, boys" moment for the otherwise successful statesman. Julian has no idea where Gallipoli is, unless they produce hash there. Which means he probably does know where Gallipoli is.

5. In some Hollywood circles it is rumoured that voices in Hugh Grant's head—"This can't fail, Hugh"—ultimately persuaded the Englishman to leave Elizabeth Hurley at home one evening and cruise the streets for £50 prostitutes. Well, your nocturnal mission did fail there, pretty boy, big time. By the way, you can bet an entire hash driveway that Julian wouldn't have left the lovely Ms. Hurley lying on the couch by herself . . .

"Cocksucker!"

BUBBLES'S INDUSTRIES

Shopping Carts and BBQs

Better Built by Bubbles

Undoubtedly, the hardest-working resident of Sunnyvale, entrepreneurial and industrious Bubbles has created a business empire with operations in the manufacturing, retail, service and recycling sectors. Diversification is the by-product of necessity, and Bubbles's determination to feed and shelter himself and his cats has spawned these multiple revenue streams. He's an old-school mogul whose success is built on hard work alone. Try spending a day in the gully retrieving dirty old shopping carts half stuck in the mud and weeds while your clothes are attacked by an army of burrs. Not easy.

Bubbles's approach differs from those of others in the park, especially Julian and Ricky, who dedicate their efforts to

getting rich quickly. But on any given day, who is most likely to have bologna or pickled eggs on hand? That's right. Bubbles. When you own a welding torch and know how to use it, the world will beat a path to your door.

Bubbles honed his welding skills on a few thousand carts before he moved on to the more glamorous world of BBQs. But, just as any great artist's supreme confidence in his abilities can turn to arrogance, and then to madness, Bubbles can also be tempted to take his work too far. A two-storey BBQ for example. Bubbles decided to call his creation the Super Doublebunk-B-Q. No one knows why. But, holy shit, it was one hell of a feat. How do you even conceive of such a thing? Imagine a BBQ that can cook several meals simultaneously. It's enough to make Randy ruin a pair of tight white pants. But build it Bubbles did, and upon its debut, Sunnyvale looked on in awe. It stood just over six feet high and would require a tall chef and extra long utensils to operate, without some sort of platform.

So why did Bubbles build the Super Doublebunk-B-Q? Well, why did Howard Hughes build the Spruce Goose? Why did Van Gogh cut off his ear? Why did the Leafs let Joe Sakic slip by them in the draft? Some questions have no answers. It's just a big fuckin' BBQ. Enjoy!

Shopping Cart Production Cycle

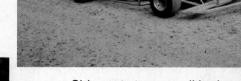

◄ Extract discarded, neglected and unattended shopping carts from the marketplace.

▲ Ship carts to reconditioning facility at Sunnyvale.

◄ Tighten the shit out of everything. Remember: little kids ride in these carts.

Ensure supply lines are always kept open. ►

◄ Take off shitty parts and replace with not-so-shitty parts.

◄ "That cocksucker's finished."

Re-market reconditioned carts to another supermarket. ►

BUBBLES'S INDUSTRIES

Kittyland Love Center, Flea Markets

Love Cats

It began as a boyhood dream for Bubbles, that one day he would open up his own daycare centre for kitties. Dare to dream, Bubbles, because Kittyland Love Center is now a reality.

Unlike dogs or fish, cats need constant attention to keep them purring along. With today's two-working-parent households, who's around to pet the little buggers or talk to them in a silly voice? Fuckin' no one, that's who. So Bubbles, being the world's greatest lover of kitties, decided he had enough love for them all. But how to provide enough stimulation for possibly hundreds of cats at a time? He built a play area that was ergonomically designed to facilitate kitty activity (this mostly consists of playing, light roughhousing and perching on tall objects to look down at things). Bubbles also included high-security chicken-wire fencing to keep the little guys from straying. It's unlikely any of the satisfied little guys would jump the three-foot fence. Cats aren't as agile as people think.

Some of Kittyland's more novel features include a min merry-go-round on which each kitty rides in its own baske and a traffic-cone mountain, which must look like a brigh orange Rockies to a cat. There's also a huge sandbox—fo playing only, guys—and a big ol' tube that's as large as th Chunnel, kitty scale. And Bubbles has added about thousand things dangling on strings, because kitties simply can't resist swatting shit with their cute little paws.

Like most daycare facilities, Bubbles's is self-funded. The fucking feds don't see the value in a well-raised kitty, someone has to bring the little buggers up right. Bubble charges just enough to cover the costs of cat food, fresh bag of sand now and then, his lot fee for the shed and bologna and bread on Thursdays. He's not getting rich, but that's okay. Just seeing the kitties happy is rewar enough. When asked if he had thoughts about franchising Kittyland Love Center, Bubbles shrugged and suggeste that most people aren't as committed to kitties as he is Plus, obtaining enough orange traffic cones is fuckin harder than you might think.

Flea Market Frenzy

You can bet that when Sunnyvale rolls out the bargain tables, there's gonna be some wild shit to be had. In the heart of this trinket tornado hustles Bubbles, who has mastered the psychological art of the flea market sale. His displays, which feature adorable kitties in mini shopping carts, hold buyers spellbound. Bubbles can name his price and move the merchandise.

Whether it's J-Roc's illicit CDs or his own re-marketed BBQs, Bubbles knows how to close the sale. Great pitches like "That cocksucker's a beauty" or "She's got less than two hundred cheeseburgers on her grill" work every time. His signature technique involves putting an outrageous price tag on his kitty-in-a-cart (last flea market, he marked it up to $40,000). Nobody purchased the priceless gem, to Bubbles's relief, but it did make the other items on his table seem like bargains.

Bubbles's continued success comes down to two simple rules. First, don't spend the money you make on other people's shit. And second, as the end of the day draws near, sell your shit for whatever people will pay. Otherwise you have to lug it all back to your shed.

Bubbles's Kitty Care Tips

Taking proper care of the park's ever-growing cat population is tough work. There's only one person who has the good nature and expertise to take on the task. When it comes to kitties, Bubbles has a heart that's bigger than his bespectacled eyeballs. "I just love the little fuckers," he says with a smile. To ensure your kitties remain healthy and happy, Bubbles recommends any responsible kitty owner does as he does.

- Give your cats names they can be proud of, like Sergeant Meowenstein, Daisy or Stinkster.
- Tickle their bellies.
- Don't let them drink garbage juice.
- Keep them away from Sam's shitty greasy hot dogs.
- Don't hire them out to guard pot plants.
- Tickle their bellies twice.
- Don't let them sleep in a shitty old car. A nice warm shed is better.
- Find a reputable kitty daycare like Kittyland Love Center.
- Make sure they get at least nineteen hours of sleep a day.
- Don't scold them if they leave dead snakes in your shoes.
- If they follow you to jail, give them extra lovin'.
- If they eat your hash, just let them sleep it off and poop it out.
- Cut the strings of tinsel hanging from their arses after Christmas. Never pull them out. Never!
- Throw any hairballs at Mr. Lahey; he could use a little extra up top.

Bubbles's Guitar Tips

- Playing with gloves is better than playing with mittens, unless you're playing just power chords.
- Before playing Rush's awesome "Overture" from *2112*, double-check that your guitar has the A, D, B and E strings, not just E and G (see photo).
- Remember that great guitar licks will always attract lots of kitties and ladies.
- "Liquor and Whores" is a heart-wrenching ballad when played on acoustic guitar.
- Remember to check the inside of your guitar for sleeping kitties, or else the sound quality really sucks.
- Don't let Ricky keep his dope inside your guitar. Dope should always be stored in the guitar case instead.

Bubbles's Samsquanch Phobia

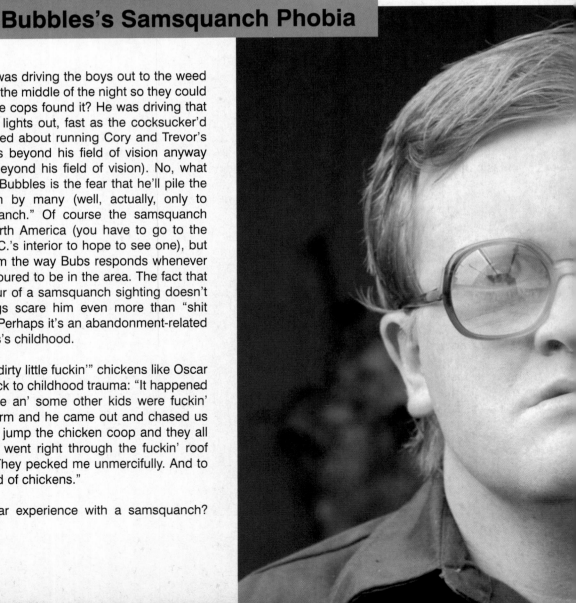

Remember when Bubbles was driving the boys out to the weed field (see "Workin' Man") in the middle of the night so they could harvest their crop before the cops found it? He was driving that van hard, bootlegger-style, lights out, fast as the cocksucker'd go. He wasn't terribly worried about running Cory and Trevor's flipped car—the wreck was beyond his field of vision anyway (Bubbles's nose sits just beyond his field of vision). No, what really freaks out our friend Bubbles is the fear that he'll pile the van into the beast known by many (well, actually, only to Bubbles) as the "samsquanch." Of course the samsquanch doesn't inhabit eastern North America (you have to go to the extensive weed fields of B.C.'s interior to hope to see one), but you wouldn't know this from the way Bubs responds whenever one of these beasts is rumoured to be in the area. The fact that Bubbles starts every rumour of a samsquanch sighting doesn't matter; these friggin' things scare him even more than "shit ropes" or Cyrus. But why? Perhaps it's an abandonment-related issue originating in Bubbles's childhood.

Certainly, his deep fear of "dirty little fuckin'" chickens like Oscar Goldman can be traced back to childhood trauma: "It happened when I was a little guy. Me an' some other kids were fuckin' around at Mr. Johnson's farm and he came out and chased us and we all ran and tried to jump the chicken coop and they all made it but I slipped and went right through the fuckin' roof right down into the coop. They pecked me unmercifully. And to this day, Ricky, I am terrified of chickens."

Did Bubbles have a similar experience with a samsquanch? We can only guess . . .

The Green Bastard . . . parts unknown.

The Many Faces of Bubbles

They say the eyes are the window to the soul. That being the case, Bubbles has a soul that is as wide as the open skies of Sunnyvale. He can clearly see what true friendship means even when his friends do their best to fuck it up. Bubbles wears his emotions on his checkered sleeves, where they seem magnified not by his glasses, but by the true spirit that resides inside.

ASK
a Trailer Park
DECORATOR

Dear Trailer Park Decorator,

I am a loyal fan of the show but I must admit that I am concerned about Bubbles's living arrangements. Does he have enough space and is he warm enough in the winter? Perhaps Bubbles doesn't pick up HGTV in his shed and therefore lacks the tools to maximize the efficiency of his limited square footage. What should he do?

Yours,
A Concerned Viewer

Dear Concerned Viewer,

The space limitations that Bubbles lives with are familiar to condo owners everywhere and his challenges are in no way unique. The good news is that, with a few simple changes, Bubbles can turn his prized shed into a "visually airy, inspirational lifestyle experience." By following our simple directions, he may not move Martha Stewart to a colour-induced, decorating orgasm, but with the right attention to organic, natural fibres and neutral paint palettes he could make her breathe a little harder.

These are the first things Bubbles needs to do:

- Paint and accessorize with monochromatic earth colours that will easily transition to the great outdoors—conveniently located not more than 10 inches from the foot of his bed.
- Choose dual-purpose, low-profile furniture that can be used for entertaining and not just sleeping, cooking or bowel evacuation. With a tone-on-tone damask over the seat, a simple toilet becomes a throne for any regal visitor!

Having said this, certain things are absolute no-nos if Bubbles wants to optimize the space he does have:

- Stay away from overstuffed furniture (sectional couches, leather club chairs).
- Avoid grand pianos, but keep that vast guitar collection—provided it exceeds no more than one shitty acoustic.
- Do not adopt really big cats like Steve French.
- Collectibles only decrease the sense of space. Bubbles's retro doe-eyed cat paintings and sepia photos of cute kitties must be grouped and limited.
- When inviting Ricky, Julian, J-Roc and others over to watch the game, never invite more than one of them—and ask this guest to bring airline-sized bottles of liquor rather than space-consuming 40-ouncers.
- A large gas fireplace is tempting for its heating qualities (Daisy and Vince the Pince would love it), but would simply take up too much space. More sweaters and thicker cat fur are the answer.
- Given that there is not enough room in this space to swing a cat (though Bubbles would never), particular care has to be given to planning the kitchen. Avoid appliances any bigger than an Easy-Bake oven.

If Bubbles follows our easy makeover plans, we could well imagine him being joined in his new home by an amorous Martha Stewart pounding the liquor and downing some delicious pickled eggs. She loves those cocksuckers.

"I am the liquor."

State-of-the-art equipment is a must for any successful surveillance operation. Here, Mr. Lahey shows off a gadget that M of the British Secret Service would be proud of. The camera is cleverly hidden inside a cooler. The chances of anyone at the park opening a cooler to see if there's cold beer inside are highly unlikely. Good plan, Jim.

CRACK SURVEILLANCE TIPS

Randy in action. Julian is caught in the act. Good job, Randy. Julian later tells him to fuck off. Randy's a pro and is unfazed.

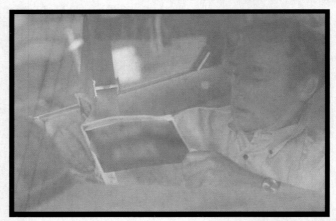

Stakeouts can take time. Avoid the boredom by bringing some good reading material.

There's no substitute for a great disguise. It allows you to slip into a scene without being detected. Is that Randy? I don't think so. It looks more like an elf who's pretending to be a male prostitute. Yup, that's gotta be it.

Always take cover behind an object that will conceal your presence. Mr. Lahey is well hidden by a full evergreen in front and Randy's full belly on his flank.

A good set of binoculars can be focused to compensate for bad eyesite and extreme drunkenness.

No matter what Julian or Mr. Lahey might say to the contrary, the real power in Sunnyvale rests with none other than park owner Barb Lahey. Who decides when the park needs a temporary relief assistant trailer park supervisor (you're out, Randy!)? Who decides on a replacement trailer park supervisor when Jim goes to jail (you're in, Ricky!)? And who cozies up to that replacement supervisor so she can win back control of the park (Do you love her, Ricky?)? As you might have guessed, she's got men problems.

The ancient principles of the yin and yang from Chinese philosophy might best describe the tempestuous relationship that exists between Barb Lahey and her on-again, off-again ex-husband. The yin typically represents the feminine side of the interaction of all the Earth's life forces (or just Barb's), while the yang represents the masculine (Jim mostly, maybe Sam Losco and a bit of Ricky, too—a powerhouse like Barb can hold up her half of this equation, even as the suitors add up over the years). When these principles exist in equal measure, harmony reigns in Sunnyvale (like at the end of season six). When a whole lot of extra yang (Randy!) throws the balance into question, you know all hell's gonna break loose (like the rest of the time).

As the park's reigning queen bee, she's got a buzzing hive of shit to worry about. But with a glint in her eye as saucy as her white cowboy boots and denim skirt, Barb's unquestionably the boss, no matter who's wearing the khaki pants, or the bee suit.

NEVER A CROWD

Come and knock on her trailer door. She's been waiting for you. Where those kisses are hers and his and his, three is company, true. Yes, life in the owner's trailer is about to get very interesting. Pragmatic Barb will have her hands full now that she's living with a couple of former roommates. Will she have the patience for lovable and unpredictable (drunk) Jim and bubbly and vivacious (hungry) Randy? Though we hear Randy keeps a pretty clean house, raking leaves, picking up trash, empty bottles . . . Jim.

The new supervisor moving in might upset the yin-yang applecart, but at least he won't increase the laundry load, just a little extra bleach to get the dirt and cheese out of those white pants. Those boys! Mind you, there's about to be a whole lot less space in the freezer, and the refrigerator's in for a shit kickin', too. Not to mention the liquor cabinet.

This arrangement seems cozy enough, but what will the rest of the park think of Barb living with two fellas? At least with Barb being the landlady, Jim and Randy won't have to assume any . . . unfamiliar positions to appease public opinion. You know what we're talking about here. We foresee years of warmth and happiness to come, an unqualified domestic success.

It's Hammered Time

Dear Trailer Park Advisors,

As I watch Jim Lahey stumble around the park trying to keep order amongst all the hooligans, I can't help but think that he might have a drinking problem. Jim's a good man trying his best under tough circumstances, but I hate to think he's becoming a drunk. Do you think he's headed for trouble?

Yours,
Concerned

Dear Concerned,

Your concern for Jim Lahey is deeply moving and frankly, with the exception of Randy, it's unprecedented. Since Lahey would never answer an AA questionnaire regarding his drinking habits (probably because his schedule is far too packed with pants-pissing activities), we thought we would complete one for him and hopefully answer your concerns.

Q: Have you ever decided to stop drinking for a week or so, but given in after a couple of days?
A: Jim Lahey is the liquor. That's just a stupid question.

Q: Do you wish people would mind their own business about your drinking and stop telling you what to do?
A: Telling Bobandy to "frig off" works like a charm.

Q: Have you ever switched from one kind of drink to another in the hope that this would keep you from getting drunk?
A: Yes. He drinks from Julian bottles and then Ricky bottles. Later on from Ray bottles. It's a great system if you're a drunk bastard and always will be.

Q: Have you had to indulge in an eye-opener upon awakening during the past year?
A: Being thrown in a pool after an all-night bender during which your car roof inexplicably gets torn clean off actually counts as an eye-closer. Stagnant, urine-tinged water stings like hell.

Q: Do you envy people who can drink without getting into trouble?
A: What?

Q: Have you had problems connected with drinking during the past year?
A: Unless repeatedly falling down your own stairs, losing your job or presiding over the "trailer park of the Apocalypse" count as problems, no, not really.

Q: Has your drinking caused trouble at home?
A: Except for that thing with Smokey the male prostitute and Jim's subsequent divorce, no, not at all.

Q: Do you ever try to get more drinks at a party because you just can't drink enough?
A: He doesn't get invited to parties. Next question.

Q: Do you tell yourself you can stop drinking any time you want to, even though you keep getting drunk when you don't always intend to?
A: Now that's just another stupid question. He always intends to get drunk.

Q: Have you missed days of work because of drinking?
A: No.

Q: Do you have blackouts?
A: Don't you?

Q: Have you ever felt that your life would be better if you did not drink?
A: Haven't we already told you? Jim Lahey IS the liquor.

We hope this helps.

All the best,
TPA

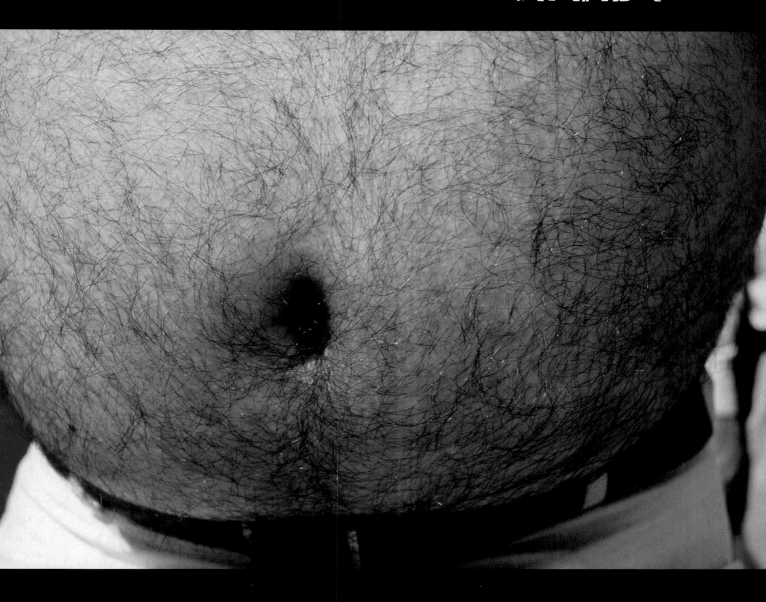

"Frig off!"

ASSISTANT TRAILER PARK SUPERVISOR DUTIES

- Assist park supervisor in maintaining law and order within the legally recognized park boundaries. Attempt to keep cheeseburger consumption to below ten per day, so as not to impede required mobility.

- Help park supervisor keep park secure and free of violence, intruders and thieves. Freely take on Ricky or Cyrus to maintain an atmosphere of safety—an assistant park supervisor must feel comfortable wrestling. If extra mobility and heart-stopping ferociousness are required, feel free to remove pants.

- Help coordinate, promote and conduct local park theatre group with park supervisor. Dress in giant bumblebee suit as required.

- Know how to get stains out of khaki pants.

- Pull over unlicensed go-karts towing or carrying unsafe loads, such as illicitly procured shopping carts or any unconscious drunks named Ricky.

- Keep persistently troublemaking residents under very strict surveillance. This duty will demand fewer trips to the grocery store to buy frozen burgers, and more time spent conducting maintenance on walkie-talkies and making quick (surveillance-based) trips to the LC.

- During fall and spring, keep grounds thoroughly raked of leaves. This job must be undertaken without a shirt on. Remember, you're beautiful.

- Discourage liquor consumption/bottle accumulation in the park that may contribute to the Bottle Kids' ever growing arsenal. In event of a Bottle Kids attack, be sure to turn off your BBQ before cleaning up any broken bottles. Safety first!

- Contribute an occasional shit analogy when shittiness of a particular shitstorm eludes shit detector of park supervisor (well done, Ricky!).

- Between mouthfuls of cheeseburgers, try suggesting to park supervisor that not pissing himself would be a good idea.

Randy recommends using a conditioner that builds body and reduces tangles.

A MAN'S GOTTA EAT

The Life of SMOKEY the Bare

The pavement is cold. The wind chills your shirtless body. Hope disappears into the pallid skies of a grey afternoon. Hunger consumes you, but you press on. And then, when another step seems futile, it hits you like the warm breath of angels come to save your starving soul: the smell of grilling cheeseburgers. Your mind races. Your mouth tingles as salivation coats your dry tongue. The promise of unrivalled pleasure is enough to drive you mad. A cold, shirtless, hungry man might do anything for that cheeseburger. And he does.

The story of shirtless men arriving in the big city with nothing but (well, without even) the shirt on their backs is not a new one. Many such lives spiral downward to tragic conclusions, thanks to the allure of grilled beef. The very thought of hot steaming meat stuffed between two warm, soft buns can break even the strongest man. Randy was strong. He broke.

Sure, he toyed with the soft, moist folds of the donair. Most men find them irresistible. But Randy's insatiable hunger could never be fully satisfied by anything but beef, straightforward grilled beef slathered in hot, oozing cheese that dribbled down his chin in his careless enthusiasm. You know what you're getting with a cheeseburger—there's nothing really to hide. The donair, meanwhile, is cloaked in a shiny wrapper, hiding its complicated ingredients inside.

It's no surprise now that Randy went the way of the cheeseburger. He would hang around burger joints and stare at patties sizzling away on the grill. Wanting to sink his teeth into every juicy one of them, he found it hard to walk away. Randy's desire for beef could only be described as an addiction, one that often left Smokey asking other men on the streets for beef as they passed him by. He's even been known to loiter outside donair shops looking for people he might swing away from the donair and convince to grab some beef with him instead. Some even say he got the nickname "Smokey" because he plied his trade redolent of the fatty smoke from the grill.

Life for men who choose the cheeseburger can be challenging. Society is quick to label them and can be callous in its assumptions about anyone who deviates from the expected. But what's the big deal? We all need to eat. Does it really matter what consenting adults choose to sink their teeth into? Whether you prefer cheeseburgers or donairs, isn't the most important thing the fact that you've found something that can hook a boy up when he needs it? Smokey understands this. Maybe others will too . . . Someday.

"Hands down, boys."

Cory and Trevor
Strip Joint Etiquette

- When dealing with peeler-bar erections that you could practically hang a towel on, try to maintain eye contact with the dancers—this will help divert their eyes away from the ridiculous beacon between your legs.

- Erections in strip bars are in bad taste. Try to avoid them by dousing yourself with cold water or slamming your fingers in the door of the Shitmobile.

- Dancers don't want to look at Cory and Trevor's huge erections—no matter how impressive they might be.

- Yes, it's ironic that erections are discouraged in places that exist only to titillate men, but there you have it. That's the fuckin' way she goes.

- Take a cue from Bubbles if you're feeling frisky: try bending over to tie your shoes until the erection goes away or you pass out.

- If you insist on having a strip-bar erection, at the very least be useful: stand by your server while she's wiping down tables so she has somewhere to hang her towels.

- Avoid ordering the chipped beef special from the businessman's lunch menu.

- Public erections do not impress Julian—and Lord knows you two want to impress him—so ease up on the boners ya boneheads!

- Keep several hand tools in your pocket to conveniently explain away the protuberant new profile of your trousers

- Try to wear really Randy-like tight pants that will keep the monster in its place.

- Track pants are a definite no-no.

- Do not go swimming in a public pool immediately after your exit from the strip joint. Wait at least one hour.

- Try not to spend too much time rearranging the extra inventory in your trousers. It might be confused with fondling, and you will be thrown out on your ass.

- When getting tossed from a strip joint because you have an erection, fall on your back.

- Any doctor who ever said that a boner couldn't fracture was a woman . . . and probably not a doctor.

Cory and Trevor The Art of Siphoning Gas

Ever since Cory and Trevor were infants sucking at their mothers' breasts, they knew that one day they would apply this rudimentary skill to a successful career in petty crime. The beauty of gas siphoning is in several ways much like that of road hockey: one, it's simple; two, all you need is a stick and a ball, or in the case of siphoning, a hose and a tank; and three, you play road hockey where cars ain't and siphon gas where cars are. So, you can see how similar the two activities are. Furthermore, road hockey is played for little or no money, and gas siphoning isn't going to buy you that winter home in Palm Springs. But it puts the occasional bag of chips on the table and a pack of smokes in your pocket and that's not too bad. But what exactly is gas siphoning? And how does it work?

Simply put, gas siphoning is the process of sucking gas out of one car, for use in another—usually Ricky's or Julian's. To do this, you place one end of a plastic tube or rubber hose in a car's tank, and feed the other end into an empty gas can positioned lower than the tank. We know gravity will cause the gas will flow downward to the gas can, but how does the gas flow upward out of the car's tank in the first place? The process begins with Cory or Trevor sucking on the hose—the end not in the car's tank—creating suction, or an air-pressure differential, between the car's tank and the gas can. Once the gas rises up, it has to flow down. Gravity takes over, and Cory or Trevor must place that loose end of the hose into the gas can right away. But why does the gas in the tank continue to "follow" the gas through the tube? This process involves something called "cohesion," in which tiny forces between the gas molecules cause them to stick together and follow one another up the tube. Consequently, just about any stupid fucker can siphon gas because it's not really them doing the work, but physics, ie. Mother Nature, right?

There's no doubt that Cory and Trevor are not sharp, so gas siphoning seems to be a suitable part-time profession. Working as a team, one stands watch while the other sucks the hose. The trick of the trade is to suck hard enough to get the gas flowing out of the tank, but not so hard that you end up swallowing a big mouthful. Any drops that do flow into your mouth, you ought to spit out. After a full day of siphoning, however, you will inevitably swallow an accidental mouthful here and there. For instance, Cory and Trevor swallowed far too many mouthfuls when Ricky and Julian started their illegal gas redistribution program. This not only landed Cory and Trevor in jail, but on oxygen to help reduce their blood octane level.

TEN THINGS/PEOPLE SMARTER THAN CORY AND TREVOR

1. Most species of insects
2. Bits of string
3. Steve French
4. Sergeant Meowenstein
5. Ray's wheelchair
6. Derek Zoolander
7. Nigel Tufnel
8. Old lottery tickets
9. Dalmations (an allegedly stupid breed but still smarter)
10. Ricky. Yes, Ricky. Ricky is smarter than combined intellects of Cory and Trevor. Maybe…

TEN THINGS/PEOPLE THAT GET MORE RESPECT THAN CORY AND TREVOR

1. Most species of insects
2. Rodney Dangerfield
3. Ralph Malph
4. The Ford Pinto
5. De-alcoholized beer
6. Spam
7. Yanni
8. Gary Coleman
9. Eight-track tape decks
10. Navel lint

TEN OCCUPATIONS CORY AND TREVOR WOULD LIKELY FAIL AT

1. Entomologists (a branch of science concerned with the study of insects)
2. Lab rats
3. Guidance counselors
4. Male models
5. Gas station attendants
6. President and Vice President of The United States (although, they couldn't do a worse job than you know who. . . .)
7. Librarians
8. Air traffic controllers
9. Editor of Sunday New York Times crossword puzzle
10. Goons in the National Hockey League

CORY AND TREVOR'S MOST DEGRADING MOMENT

In season four's "Workin' Man" episode, Ricky forcibly packs Cory and Trevor into a not-so-big courier shipping box to act as drug mules (minus the bag of potato chips that Ricky has confiscated from them).

CORY AND TREVOR ON THEIR RELATIONSHIP WITH THE BOYS

"I dunno, I don't want to be all sentimental and gooey and stuff but, I love the guys. And I think they sincerely love us too," Cory says of his relationship with Ricky and Julian.

Now, contrast this with how Ricky views Cory and Trevor: "If any shit goes down, it'll be Cory and Trevor taking the heat, not us. That's why we usually work with Cory and Trevor, because THEY go to jail instead of us, which is perfect."

Dogs versus Cory and Trevor
Who's Smarter And Makes A Better Pet?

Just how smart are Cory and Trevor when compared to man's best friend? According to conventional wisdom, the funnier-sounding the name of the dog, the more likely it is to be smarter than Sarah's whipping boys. Which pets deserve a place in the home of Sarah and Lucy, or to be allowed "on the job" with the boys? Let's see how they match up.

Cockapoo versus Cory and Trevor

The cockapoo is an easily trained dog of extraordinary intelligence, wonderful disposition, abounding affection and little to no shedding or "doggy" odour. Cory and Trevor do exhibit abounding affection for the boys, but we are not sure how they fare in the shedding or odour departments. As for the intelligence . . . just look at how smart this dog looks, and how not-smart Cory and Trevor look. This is a tough contest: cockapoos are brainy, but they are next to useless when it comes to harvesting weed. Cory and Trevor are much less demanding, but they still need to be fed and walked daily.
Winner: Slight edge to Cory and Trevor.

Pekingese versus Cory and Trevor

The Pekingese is a well-balanced, compact dog of Chinese origin. Its temperament is one of directness, independence and individuality. The breed combines aristocratic dignity with intelligence and self-importance to make for a happy but really opinionated pet (don't get it started on politics or religion). It is a good companion to those who earn its respect. We are pretty sure Cory and Trevor are not of Chinese origin, and that should not be held against them, but the dignity thing is an issue: it turns out a Pekingese has loads of the stuff, and our boys possess, precisely, less than none. On the positive side for Cory and Trevor, Pekingese do not have opposable thumbs, nor is the breed tall enough to reach the sink; therefore, they can't do Sarah and Lucy's dishes. Cory and Trevor, on the contrary, perform household duties very well.
Winner: One has dignity, the other does dishes, so it's a tie.

Chihuahua versus Cory and Trevor

Kennel clubs contend that chihuahuas are graceful, alert, swift-moving little dogs that delight owners with a "saucy expression." Quite frankly, we wouldn't give a shit if these rat-like dog wannabes found a cure for cancer or confirmed the existence of God: a chihuahua is still a chihuahua.
Winner: Cory and Trevor win this contest paws down.

Pug versus Cory and Trevor

Generally considered a well-mannered, even-tempered breed, exhibiting stability, playfulness, great charm, dignity and an outgoing, loving disposition, the pug is reputed to be smarter than humans who answer to the names "Cory" and "Trevor." We don't think there is any question whatsoever that Cory and Trevor are even tempered, but beyond this, the pug wins in most departments—particularly with the dreaded dignity issue popping up again. Strange as it sounds, small, yappy dogs seem to have dignity to spare. They have no good reason to share the sort of dignity that bigger breeds enjoy, but they do, almost as if they have no idea how they're perceived by others (we're talking about small, yappy dogs here, not Cory and Trevor). We can't help but respect this kind of confidence. Despite its wingless-bat appearance, this dog seems to take the lead. But let's not forget a few key points: a pug is next to useless during a holdup; its ridiculous little paws can't grasp automatic weapons, nor can they pull nylon tights over its absurd, mushed-up face; and their short legs cannot be held up in the air for an unrequited handshake, or propel its tiny body quickly enough for a getaway. We're starting to have a change of heart here.
Winner: Cory and Trevor—crap in a heist, but a pug would be a downright liability.

Pomeranian versus Cory and Trevor

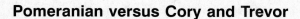

The Pomeranian is an extrovert, exhibiting great intelligence and vivacious spirit. It has attitude to spare, a luxuriant double coat of fur and can wear dog clothes with real style, making it a great companion for anybody with a subscription to *GQ*. In the grooming department, there's no competition: Trevor's mullety mop of hair cannot hope to compete with this breed, nor can Cory's Willie Nelson braids. As for brains, we already know the answer to this one (in puppy school, these dogs get straight A's). It's a tighter contest when comparing their relative physiques. Pomeranians weigh an average four to six pounds, and are therefore a bit lighter than Cory and Trevor combined. The bottom line is this: the dog is pretty wimpy. Bubbles's cat Vince the Pince could kick the shit out of this fancypants pooch with one deformed paw tied behind his back. How Cory and Trevor would fair in a scrap with this stylish canine, however, is almost too close to call.
Winner: Cory and Trevor, only because they can siphon gas.

The overall edge goes to Cory and Trevor. Oh sure, these two may fuck up almost every job they're ever given, but they ask very little in return—only an occasional scratch on the belly from Sarah, some food and Jiffy Wine, and, from time to time, a shake of their paws by their masters Ricky and Julian. So cancel that call for a pick-up from the dog pound, we think these two should be allowed to stay. Ricky did "raise Cory and Trevor" to become a trailer park's best friend, after all.

TRAILER PARK BOYS
Postcards from the Park

Free at last, free at last, Bubbles is free of that dirty 'ol cocksucker tooth at last.

Hark, what light through window breaks? It is the sun and Ricky, the passed out drunk.

Ricky returns from shopping at J-Roc's. He paid for the merchandise with the "You used my dope money to buy this shit" card.

50% representin' in the hood, 50% arthritic hand puppetry.

What? You think Julian's the only guy in the park with style?

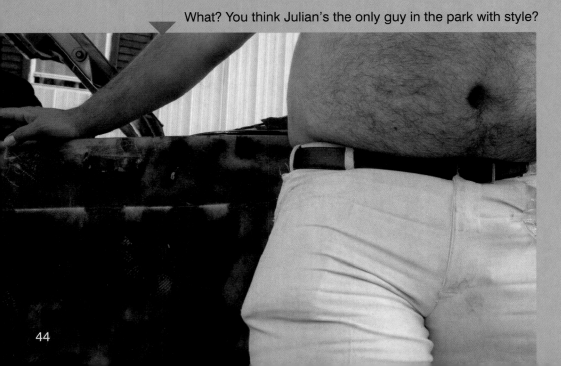

"NOMESAYIN"

The Unwrapping of J-Roc and T

It doesn't take a nomecensus of human history to know that many turning points in world affairs were brought about by seemingly insignificant events that no one would ever have guessed could change the world. Cases in point:

It could have been the pickled eggs or maybe it was just a bad chicken finger; whatever the cause, Bubs's tooth ache became abscessed and before you could say "fuckface" that wack bastard Conky was back in town.

One of the most insignificant hydro outages in North American history occurred one Christmas eve in Sunnyvale when a drunken, Grinch-like Mr. Lahey threw the main power switch in the park. Insignificant? Think again. While putting a pop/rock album on the record player, a well-mannered young lad named Jamie asks his pal, Tyler, if he has ever "tried marijuana." The air is even less thick with attitude than it is with purple haze. Suddenly the lights go out and the turntable needle scratches to a halt. It's a revelation. These two sheltered young fans of 4/4 time, stringed instruments and drums you don't plug in remark only that this sound is "pretty cool." But we can almost see the essences of Tyler and Jamie pack up their vests and corduroys and leave Sunnyvale for good—only to return

briefly in moments of great weakness and vulnerabilit (thanks, DVS). In their places, J-Roc and T were two bun in they baby-momma oven, becomin' the rhymin freestylin' mafuckas they was meant to be, nomesayin?

The name "J-Roc" is multi-dimensional. The first part, "J unto itself is not much of a handle and could be confused with "Jay," which by itself is low on the cool scale. Bu when "J" is used in partnership with another word, explodes with possibilities—JD, JFK, JJ (Kid Dyn-o-mite) "Roc" is good by itself. It's hard as "fuc" right? But put it with "J" and it gets even harder. Harder than J-Roc's . . (see Microphone Assassin episode for details).

Now "T" is a very versatile moniker. Naturally it derive from the name Tyrone, but it could represent other qualitie in the man, including "T"errified, when Steve French cam to visit; "T"ee'd off, by J-Roc's overuse of "nomesayin' "T"ricky, when he tried to fool Ricky about using the dop money for sound gear.

Shakespeare asked, "What's in a name?" For J-Roc and T just the right letters. Peace out.

Great look here for J-Roc. Is that the official toque of the
Compton Jr. Hosers minor hockey team?

Apocalypse J-Roc.

That lumber jacket look would kick ass at a Helix concert.

J-Roc may think he's black. The sun's UV rays have a

TRAILER PARK BOYS
Postcards from the Park

Ah, the good 'ol days with a little rooftop drinkin'. Before Mr. Lahey's drinkin' led to the mysterious disappearance of the rooftop.

Who ever thought cool ice blue could be so HOT!

Conky's the one on Bubbles's right. Bubbles is the other one.

Poor Julian. At least it's not raining. In fact it never rains at Sunnyvale.

Cory's thinking, "Does Sarah want to bang me?" Sarah's thinking, "I bet Cory will clean my trailer." Trevor's just not thinking.

"Just because we look after them
doesn't mean we're bangin' them."

The Lovely Sarah

. . . and the Elusive Art of Happiness

Regular observers of life in Sunnyvale will notice that most of the park inhabitants lead fairly uncomplicated, satisfied and relatively happy lives, provided the following conditions are met: the kitties are warm and well fed; J-Roc is flush with scrilla to spend on his baby mamas; Randy and Mr. Lahey are free to explore experimental theatre; and the boys are allowed to smoke and drink. Everybody is happy—everybody except the lovely Sarah. Let's face facts: living with Ricky's girlfriend and daughter can put the weight of the world on a girl's tattooed shoulders. Every day Sarah is forced to be a den mother, babysitter, bouncer (Ricky!), negotiator (Julian!), pet trainer (Cory and Trevor) . . . the list goes on. We know that deep inside Sarah's a fun-loving sweetheart—she genuinely cares for Trinity and Lucy, and no one has ever had cause to report her treatment of Cory and Trevor to the Humane Society—but she can't help but go through life with the proverbial stone in her shoe or bee in her trucker's cap. Thinking we could brighten her day, we compiled a list of things that we hope will bring a smile back to Sarah's face.

Things That Might Make Sarah Happy

1. The Sunnyvale Kennel Club hosting a contest of local canine talent at which Cory and Trevor win Best in Show. She would be happy. Maybe even thrilled.

2. B 9—"Bingo!"

3. Hearing the news that tattoos are now covered by the provincial health-care plan.

4. An IOC announcement that hash hockey is going to be a demonstration sport at the Beijing Summer Olympics, along with the request that she and Lucy lead the Canadian team.

5. You might be excused for thinking that Cory and Trevor painting her toenails would make her happy. This is just one of the many duties that Sarah expects of them, and it gives her little, if any, additional pleasure (although we suspect she loves watching them take out the garbage).

6. A bottle, a joint and a willing Julian.

7. Winning a lifetime supply of animal-print designer wear from the Animal Print Sweepstakes would be better than winning the lottery for lovely Sarah. Nothing says happiness like faux leopard spots.

THE STYLE OF SARAH AND LUCY

This spring, top offerings from the design houses of Paris, London and New York will not be on display around Sunnyvale. Instead, we can look forward to an exciting season of animal prints of almost limitless variety—indeed, rumour has it that Sarah's wardrobe contains more jaguar-print skirts than there are actual jaguars remaining in the wild. (It's a wonder Bubbles can keep his hands off of her.) Unquestionably, this is a woman who knows how to push the envelope of print design to create a look and style all her own. And you know she'll accentuate every pattern to its maximum advantage with ankle bracelets, new tattoos, navel jewellery and haute couture baseball caps featuring Peterbilt and Western Star logos to give her look just a little bit of sass.

If she opts for a cheeky mauve jaguar-print skirt (not designed by Yves Saint Laurent), we can expect her to accessorize with a limited-edition faux Gucci bag that is both practical—big enough to carry Cory and Trevor's water dish—and elegant enough for a trip to the kebab shop or the LC. Watch for her to accent skin-tight skirts with even tighter tube tops featuring trendy colours like Easy Orange and Fat-Wallet Green.

This season Lucy will make a big splash with a playfully cropped, fish-net, mauve top that manages to pull off that tricky balancing act of radiating trampy allure during the daytime without seeming an outright sure thing in the evening. Her choice of slacks will invariably rely upon the elegant camel-toe cut that Audrey Hepburn made so famous in the late fifties. This style draws attention to the garment's focal point while still managing to maintain a hint of class. Lucy will feel extra saucy in a black push-up bra that says "come and get me big boy" (Julian), while maintaining a hard-to-get, "piss off" look (Ricky). It's bitchy couture at its finest. Add to the mix breezy blonde hair the colour of Saskatchewan wheat, coupled with earthen brown roots the colour of . . . well . . . dirt, and Lucy will be the talk of the Sunnyvale's gravel runway this season.

And remember: Barbie pink is the new black.

I LOVE LUCY

Is it a coincidence that two of the most beloved couples in television history happen to share the same names? But, really, how similar are our Lucy and Ricky to THE Lucy and Ricky? (You remember, Lucy McGillicuddy and Ricky Ricardo of *I Love Lucy*.) As it turns out, these couples share many qualities.

Ricky versus Ricky

- Both Rickys have wonderfully styled hair.
- Both Rickys speak English—although, both Rickys not so well.
- Both Rickys enjoy a good smoke—cigars, cigarettes, weed.
- Both Rickys like big, powerful bands: Cuban swing; Helix.
- Both Rickys have really cool friends. Bubbles and Fred Mertz are virtually clones.
- Both Rickys love Lucy—except when Lucy screwed up Ricky's show or Lucy screwed Officer George Green.
- We think one of the Rickys may have yelled out "I love Lucy" during sex. It was probably Ricky.
- One said "Babaloo" and the other "Bobandy"—close enough.
- One changes at the club and then performs. The other performs with a club to get change (parking meters).
- They both love the hot Latin taste of jalapeno.

Lucy versus Lucy

- Both Lucys wear sexually suggestive outfits. Lucy tends to wear sleazy frocks with matching purses and trampy shoes, while Lucy opts for short skirts with sleazy boots.
- Both like to get wasted from time to time. Remember when Lucy got into the Vitameatavegamin and got really hammered? She practically got it on with Fred right on screen after that one . . .
- Both have really cool best friends. Sarah and Ethel Mertz are virtually clones of one another.
- We think that one of the Lucys may have yelled out "Ohhhhhhhh Ricky" during sex. It was probably Lucy.
- Both Lucys are drawn to show business, whether it means appearing at The Club or in a J-Roc film.

Sure, Lucy's a ball-breaker at times, but let's face it, Ricky's no treat either. Is the guy ever around? In the end, though, they all seem to make it work. Whether it's bangin' in the back seat of the Shitmobile or straying from the sanctity of twin beds, Ricky seems to find a way to love Lucy and so do we.

"The way she goes, boys, the way she goes."

RAY AND THE THING UP THERE

RAY ON CALVINISM

Don't let the Confederate flag flying from the stolen wheelchair fool you (nor the ability to drink Nicolas Cage's character in *Leaving Las Vegas* under the table), Ray is a deep thinker. He subscribes to the Christian doctrine of Calvinism, created by the French-born, Swiss Protestant church reformer John Calvin (1509-1564). Calvinism's central doctrine is the concept of predestination, under which certain souls (the elect) are predestined by God to salvation, and the rest to damnation. We wonder if Calvinism says anything about irony: Ray, living in an old sleeper cab in a garbage dump, strikes us as leaning heavily towards being seated with the "damned" and not so much towards his inclusion at the coveted "elect" table at the Calvinist party.

The following exchange between Ray and Ricky exemplifies the intellectual depth that characterizes their father-son relationship. Particularly impressive is Ricky's use of the Socratic method (the use of questions, as employed by Socrates, to develop an idea) during Ray's explanation of Calvinism to the camera.

"I'm a Calvinist when it comes to love. Tammy was my love. I was graced by love. I hope and pray that Ricky is, but if he's not, God bless his soul, there's nothing he can do about it. That's predestination. Some people might think that this is awfully cruel, but that's life."—Ray

"Dad . . . what in the fuck are you talkin' about?"—Ricky
"I'm talkin' about predestination, for Christ's sake. You know, predestination! Love. Calvin. Grace."—Ray
"Where's my pepperoni?"

RICKY, RAY AND THE BIBLE

Unlike the other residents of Sunnyvale, Ray exudes a profound sense of inner peace. He keeps rolling along through life, the wheels of his chair absorbing each and every pothole. Perhaps this serenity comes from his keen connection with the messages contained in the Bible. That, or his consuming the best part of a 40-ouncer of vodka. Whatever the combination, it works for Ray. It's a lesson to all, that contentment can be found in a good dose of spirit.

"Who in the fuck was that jackass?"—Ricky looking at the bible pimp, Hampton
"He's not a jackass, Ricky. I just bought a bible from him to give to you. It's an everlasting gift of love to my son."—Ray
"Dad, are you drunk?"

THE WAY OF THE ROAD

We've all seen these strange, filthy bits of litter, scattered along the highway shoulder or in the ditch. Sometimes they're old wiper fluid containers, bleaching out in the hot sun, but just as often they're faded pop bottles full of what appears to be apple drink. You ask yourself, why are people throwing out perfectly good bottles of apple cola? Then you think, apple cola? What the fuck is that? Is this just the latest sugary, shitty soft drink? Maybe it doesn't taste so good, so folks are chucking it out the window? And then it slowly dawns . . . hey, that's not apple cola, and it's definitely not wiper fluid. it's . . . piss! Yes, piss—and it's the way of the road.

In Episode 3 of Season 6 Bubbles does society a great service with what amounts to a public exposé of the piss-jug problem—faced not only by Sunnyvale, but across the whole country. The Trans-Canada Highway might need to be renamed the Piss-Jug Expressway. If you don't really think there is a piss-jug crisis, at least in Sunnyvale, maybe Bubbles's explanation will convince you:

Ray used to be on the road as a trucker and here's what truckers do: they're driving along and they've got deadlines to meet. They don't want to pull in and park their truck, walk in and take a pee in the toilet and go back out and get on the road. They just have an old jug and put their bird into it and have a pee, cap it off once it's full and drill the fuckin' thing out on the highway. I don't agree with it, but I see where they are coming from to make their deadlines. Ray's been firing them all over the park like he's still driving a truck."

Ray comfortably employs this method of emptying his bladder, and piss jugs hang from Sunnyvale's trees like so much ripe fruit; there are so many of them marking the highways and byways of the park, Ricky and Bubbles have to hoist multiple jugs hung on hockey sticks slung over their shoulders to haul them all away. If they freshened up and got some braided, blonde pigtails, we'd have ourselves a couple of Bavarian piss-jug milkmaids. Actually, only Randy and Lahey would dress up like Bavarian milkmaids—but you get the idea.

Piss jugs. They may be the way of the road, but they're still fuckin' gross.

PISS JUGS: Dos and Don'ts

DO use a container with a tightly sealing cap.

DO make sure the jug has no leaks or holes, except of course for the hole in the top.

DO dispose of all full jugs before picking up a hot hitchhiker.

DO separate piss jugs from beer before embarking on a bender.

DO fill your jug like you fill a gas tank, by putting the hose right in the hole.

DON'T try to use a jug that's almost full. Disaster awaits.

DON'T begin filling the jug on a twisty road.

DON'T take chances on any container that holds less than a gallon.

DON'T use any jugs without handles, as they can slip from your grip as they get heavier.

DON'T eat and smoke while pissing and driving, you simply do not have enough hands.

DON'T watch your fill. Keep your eyes on the road.

TRAILER PARK BOYS
Postcards from the Park

Heist Rule #421: always use a land line, particularly when you can't afford a cell phone.

Did someone misplace their valium?

Where there's Smokey there's fire.

Geez, you guys steal BBQs, gas, Christmas trees, lawn furniture...how 'bout a snowblower for Bubs?

Who built Stonehenge? Where is the lost city of Atlantis? What the fuck happened to Jim's roof?

THE EPISODES

WARNING

The following section contains a review of the forty-five episodes from the first six seasons and one really messed up Christmas special. This much mayhem coming together at the same time may create a universal imbalance that could totally fuck us up but good. If it does...sorry, the way she goes.

TRAILER PARK BOYS
Postcards from the Park

Who knows what evil lurks in the hearts of men? Bubbles knows.

The sign isn't the only thing getting hammered today.

Are there NO seatbelt laws in Nova Scotia?

A gritty and nutritious urban breakfast always begins with Cheeri Hos.

For the boys "the lowest price is the law," especially when you're breaking it.

SEASON 1

Title: TAKE YOUR LITTLE GUN AND GET OUT OF MY TRAILER PARK

Air Date: APRIL 22, 2001

Writers: Mike Clattenburg, John Paul Tremblay, Robb Wells, Barrie Dunn
Director: Mike Clattenburg
Guest Stars: Jacob Rolfe (Jacob), Bernard Robichaud (Cyrus)

After a grainy flashback to Ricky and Julian in a shootout with person unknown, we join them at the Van Allen Correctional Centre—home for the past eighteen months. Julian explains to a documentary film crew that leaving jail today will be a great opportunity to turn his life around; he's had enough of petty crime and he's heading back to the trailer park to a good, clean future. Oh, and he's going to stay clear of Ricky.

Ricky proudly announces that as soon as he's out, he's "going to get really drunk." When told that Julian blames him for getting them into jail, he replies, "Julian can frig off if that's what he is telling you, 'cause it's not my fault. It's Julian's fault he went to jail. He's the one force feeding me drugs and every other goddamn thing. It's not my fault. Besides, the counsellors told me it's society's fault, it's not my fault I went to jail three times."

"Frig off, Randy."

Fast-forward to Sunnyvale Trailer Park, where mustachioed park supervisor Jim Lahey and his bare-bellied assistant Randy blame Ricky and Julian for ruining the park. Minutes later Ricky arrives and soon they're breaking up a scuffle between him and a teenage boy who refuses to cough up smokes. Jim asks after Julian's whereabout and Ricky replies, "At the Fuck Off Hotel, Lahey."

Julian returns to find his trailer filthy and the witless Cory and Trevor smoking weed on his couch. A gun-toting thug called Cyrus is now squatting in Julian's home, they say, and even Lahey is petrified of him. For his part, Cyrus claims Julian lost the privileges to his home when he went to "con college." Cyrus flashes a 9-mm handgun that his old man gave him in grade seven, and its safety is "always off."

The key Sunnyvale residents appear in turn (except Ray, who shows up in Episode 2): J-Roc, Sunnyvale's white, wannabe rapper; Julian's buddy Bubbles; Lucy (Ricky's ex and his daughter's mom) and Sarah, Lucy's roommate. Bubbles succinctly describes Cyrus for Julian: "Cocksucker." Somebody has to go, and it ain't going to be the sharp looking guy in the black T-shirt holding a rum and cola. Julian confronts Cyrus, but Cyrus won't shoot. Julian grabs the gun away and declares the park "my family." That night, feeling badly about homeless Ricky sleeping on his porch, Julian offers him a blanket, vodka and a pack of hot dogs. "Sleep in my car," he says, but only for two days. A grateful Ricky replies, "No more than two weeks. I promise."

Cyrus—Mr. Safety-off—is one dirty dog whose bark is worse than his bite.

nomesayin

REASONS TO STAY AT THE FUCK OFF HOTEL

1. Liquor and whores
2. Complimentary jalapeno chips
3. Mini-bar is maxi
4. 3-for-1 films of an adult nature
5. Guests get free pepperoni on pillow
6. Refundable piss jugs
7. Accepts empties for payment

rare photo
Julian returns to the comfort of his trailer. Ricky, to the comfort of Julian's car.

Julian's the big dog at Sunnyvale.

RICKYISM

"Look, I need some stuff and I could just rob ya or you could just give it to me, it's up to yourselves."
—Ricky, upon his release from jail, being brutally honest with a variety store clerk

Cory and Trevor can get drinks for Sarah and Lucy in peace now that Cyrus has been kicked out of the park.

BAD BOYS SCALE

	Very little. Lahey stone-cold sober. Julian sips on a little rum.
	Cory and Trevor introduce themselves to the camera as they do hot-knives.
	Cyrus does a lot of gun waggin' and braggin' but no taggin'.

SEASON 1 EPISODE 2

Title: FUCK COMMUNITY COLLEGE, LET'S GET DRUNK AND EAT CHICKEN FINGERS

Air Date: APRIL 29, 2001

Writers: Mike Clattenburg, John Paul Tremblay, Robb Wells, Barrie Dunn
Director: Mike Clattenburg
Guest Stars: George Green (Officer George Green), Jeremiah Sparks (Joey)

Julian shares a peaceful moment with his two friends rum and cola, the only ones in the park that aren't hounding him for something.

nomesayin

We hear, for the first time in the series, the disembodied voice (rumour has it that his name is Donny) that screams out from the distance from time to time. In this instance, he politely asks Ricky at the top of his lungs to "Stop fuckin' firing!" and to "Shut the fuck up!"

Julian is studiously researching his community college options—meat cutter, electrician, broadcasting—when gunfire interrupts. Outside he finds Ricky shooting and complaining that he can't sleep in the car with all the pesky insects and barking dogs. Julian takes his gun back and urges a little common sense: "THINK, RICKY, THINK!"

The next morning, Bubbles wakes Ricky and demands the return of his kitty. Ricky refuses; the cat is protecting the juvenile pot plants in the back seat from being pissed on by squirrels. Bubbles insists that the cat was merely "a loaner" and adds, "No cat of mine is going to live in a car"—although Ricky living in a broken-down New Yorker doesn't seem to bother him in the slightest.

Inside, Julian's answering machine is aglow with messages from Lucy and Lahey, both demanding his immediate attention to Ricky's latest misadventures. Looking out his window, drink in hand, Julian watches Bubbles and Ricky in what may be the most inept fight in a long history of really inept fights. Then Lucy, Lahey, Cory and Trevor begin pounding on his door. He snaps, and fires his gun into the air. He's had enough. He's leaving the park.

"Think, Ricky, Think!"

Almost. Julian signed a twenty-four-month lease and owes Lahey $1,600 in site fees. Furthermore, Lahey won't let him leave without taking Ricky, who doesn't help matters by saying "Look, I know you're stressed out, but don't worry about it, 'cause, we're going to get drunk and eat chicken fingers—me, you and the old man." Julian's not impressed and he warns Ricky: no blues music and no Ray (Ricky's dad) on his front lawn. Ricky takes this to heart and immediately invites Ray over to Julian's front lawn. When greeted by the joyous sight of a drunken father (in a stolen wheel-chair, adorned with flags celebrating the Confederacy and pirates) and a drunken son (listening to blues), Julian kicks them off his property.

Contrite, Julian offers Ricky the New Yorker to keep, so they head into town to steal parts for the car. Officer George Green catches them red handed, but Ricky talks their way out of arrest by explaining that they are all being filmed for a police training video.

The episode wraps up with Ricky getting the car to run again, impressing Lucy and Trinity. Lahey cuts Julian a deal, agreeing to waive all outstanding site fees if he'll stay—a moment Randy quietly concludes by telling Julian he's glad he's staying.

rare photo

Ricky reclines in the front seat of his new home.

Ray and Ricky, chicken fingers and blues, father and son, gettin' drunk. Good times.

RICKYISMS

"Easy there, Magnum PEI"
—Ricky to an aggressive Officer George Green

"You can go to college and get your 'PFD' or whatever the fuck it's called."
—Ricky to Julian

Ricky's solution to Sunnyvale's barking dog problem.

BAD BOYS SCALE

 Ricky gets wasted and passes out in the middle of the road.

 Ricky has four small pot plants growing in his back seat.

 Ricky and Julian both fire off a lot of rounds.

SEASON 1 EPISODE 3

Ricky has the look of a star, even if a porn star and film star are not the same.

nomesayin

Both Sarah and Lucy say Ricky is pretty good in the sack. Ricky and Bubbles's official Russian police uniforms for the porno include shoulder patches and hats that read "Security" in English.

MR. LAHEY'S SHIT ANALOGIES

"Don't forget, you started this shitstorm, Limpy."—Lahey to Ricky, upon refusing to give his porno tape back.

Title: MR. LAHEY'S GOT MY PORNO TAPE!
Air Date: MAY 6, 2001

Writers: Mike Clattenburg, John Paul Tremblay, Robb Wells, Barrie Dunn
Director: Mike Clattenburg
Guest Stars: Linda Busby (J-Roc's Mom), Angelique Jensen (Stacy), Tara Doyle (Victoria)

When Randy discovers that Ricky is growing dope in his car, he calls Lahey in for backup on the bust. Lahey arrives to see the two less-than-rock-hard men chasing each other hopelessly in circles. Once the "fight" is broken up, Lahey calls Ricky a "small-time loser." The insult really hits home. Later, J-Roc tells a broke and depressed Ricky that if he wants to make some quick cash, he should head on over to J-Roc's mom's crib.

Julian smells a rat. Sure enough, the money would come from starring in a porno film. Ricky really needs the money and decides, "I'm going to be a film star." Julian cautions that being a porn star is not the same as being a film star, but Ricky struggles with this: "There's not much of a difference—it's still film."

"Randy and I are practising for a play."

From Russia With the Love Bone tells the story of two sensitive young Russian women who run afoul of the law and must compromise their virtue in order to extricate themselves from the iron grip of authority. Bubbles is Sergeant Alexei, opposite Ricky's Sergeant Boris, who, together, represent the repressive nature of Moscow bureaucracy. Cory and Trevor describe the plot succinctly: "It's basically just a lot of sex, really."

Ricky worries Lucy will mind him doing this and his performance is wooden in every respect—except where it matters—despite the ladies' romantic overtures on bended knee. Trevor announces, "Testical difficulty, please stand by." Bubbles begs Ricky to continue: "I don't get that many chances . . . LET'S GO!" But J-Roc's mom crashes the set (yanking him out by his ear: "Ah, Mom, that hurts!") and Lahey confiscates the tape. Bubbles is left high, dry and frisky when the ladies depart, angry and unpaid. Then Lucy catches wind of Ricky's "work" and calls him a "porno gigolo," to which he responds, "I guess she took it the wrong way."

That evening, Julian sneaks into Lahey's trailer and finds Randy laying face down on a pommel horse and zipped into a leather bondage mask being attended to by a Marilyn Monroe look-alike in a little black dress. They pronounce in stunningly convincing feminine tones, "I'm not Randy" and "I'm not Mr. Lahey." Julian assures them he'll say they were "practising for a play"—if he gets the tape back. He takes the video to a grateful Ricky, and lends him a few bucks.

rare photo
Must be another J-Roc casting call at Sunnyvale.

Best fight since the Thrilla In Manila. Ricky versus Randy in the battle of the rope-a-dopes.

"The whole idea of it has got me pretty damn frisky, too. It's been quite a while since that stuff went on with me. I'm really frisky!"
—Bubbles on the prospect of having sex with the blonde "actress" in J-Roc's movie

"I'm going to make a hundred and sixty bucks. That'll buy a lot of fuckin' cat food."
—Bubbles on porno payday

"The irony is I'm doing this for my girlfriend, and if she ever found out, she'd kill me. I can't say I'd blame her. I'm a fuckin' moron."
—Ricky explaining his reasons for doing a porno

RICKYISM

"What comes around is all around!"

—Ricky, trying to explain the concept of karma to Lahey

◀ Ricky's got a slight edge, but Randy hasn't taken his pants off yet.

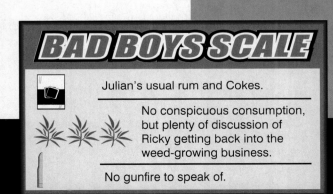

BAD BOYS SCALE

Julian's usual rum and Cokes.

No conspicuous consumption, but plenty of discussion of Ricky getting back into the weed-growing business.

No gunfire to speak of.

Mamas, don't let your babies grow up to be soundmen.

nomesayin

MR. LAHEY'S SHIT ANALOGIES

"The old shitliner is coming to port; I'll be there to tie her up." —Lahey to Ricky

Title: MRS. PETERSON'S DOG GETS FUCKED UP
Air Date: MAY 13, 2001

Writers: Mike Clattenburg, John Paul Tremblay, Robb Wells, Barrie Dunn
Director: Mike Clattenburg
Guest Stars: Sam Tarasco (Sam Losco), Craig Wood (Tractor Man), Alma Godwin (Mrs. Peterson), Jarrett Murphy (Soundman)

Julian (talking into the mirror as he shaves, smokes and eats a banana) explains that his day will be spent looking after a dog. Sparky belongs to his neighbour Mrs. Peterson, a lovely old lady who thinks Julian is her grandson. She invites him to dinner once a week, worries about his drinking and bakes him cookies. "It's like having a real grandmother," he says fondly. "It's awesome." Julian and Sparky start the day peacefully enough, then Ricky calls. He's fighting with Lucy and needs a lift to buy some dope. Julian agrees to the ride, but only if Ricky watches Sparky later while Julian runs some errands. Deal.

"Get out of the trailer, you're bleeding all over the place."

Later, at Ray's, Ricky explains the economic benefits of selling weed brownies. While rummaging for a baking sheet, Ricky finds a long-forgotten handgun. He fires it into the ceiling, confirming that it still works, and gets back to baking. Cory and Trevor arrive looking for weed, and for the first time we see Ricky bumming smokes from the hapless pair: "Smokes, let's go . . . Give a couple to her, too [pointing at Trinity]." As Ricky tries to get rid of Cory and Trevor, Sparky gets into the brownies and Trinity, checking out the pistol, accidentally shoots her dad in the ass ("Sorry, Ricky."). "You see what happens when you frig around with guns?" chides Ray.

As always, they call Julian to fix things. His friends Levi and Desiree set him up with a shady veterinarian, Sam Losco, to see to both Sparky's buzz and Ricky's wounded ass. Sam agrees to help, but only if the boys do him a favour: steal an expensive riding mower from a neighbour who owes Sam money. Mid-robbery, the owner appears with a shotgun and Ricky gets shot again. (God, it sucks when that happens.) The sound guy also gets hit and Julian yells out, "Hold your fire, somebody's been hurt here!" They scramble into the car and dump the soundman on the ER doorstep, but Julian insists on taking Ricky back to the vet (no cops involved).

Julian's day ends with a birthday present from Mrs. Peterson, who gives him the new N.W.A rap CD, and another lecture about his drinking. He also receives a phone message from the grateful sound guy, asking Julian to put in a good word with his producers, because his recovery will take four to six weeks: "Don't let them fire me. This is the best job I've ever had."

rare photo
Careful, Ricky. You don't want to get shot for a third time today.

Waiting for shit to happen.

RICKYISM

"Sam's got this thing like a calculator that can send messages all over the world."
—Ricky

"Ricky, it's the Internet."
—Julian

◀ Julian promises Mrs. Peterson he'll cut back on the drinking. Less mix.

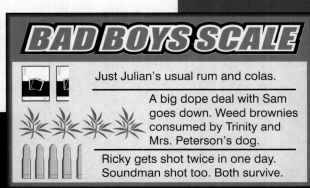

BAD BOYS SCALE

Just Julian's usual rum and colas.

A big dope deal with Sam goes down. Weed brownies consumed by Trinity and Mrs. Peterson's dog.

Ricky gets shot twice in one day. Soundman shot too. Both survive.

SEASON 1 EPISODE 5

Trevor and Cory mistakenly tell the park Ricky and Julian are gay after seeing them hug. It's not like Trevor and Cory to fuck up.

nomesayin

Ricky isn't the only television character to have a mid-life crisis about his sexuality. Remember in the movie *M*A*S*H* there was a dentist named Captain Walter "Painless Pole" Waldowski? He decides to kill himself after failing to perform and concludes that he must be gay. He's "cured" of his condition by Lieutenant Maria "Dish" Schneider later that evening. George Costanza from Seinfeld also had doubts from time to time—"It moved"—when he had a massage performed by a male masseur.

Title: I'M NOT GAY. I LOVE LUCY...WAIT A SECOND, MAYBE I AM GAY

Air Date: MAY 20, 2001

Writers: Mike Clattenburg, John Paul Tremblay, Robb Wells, Barrie Dunn
Director: Mike Clattenburg
Guest Stars: Aaron Armstrong (Police Officer)

Julian opens by explaining that Ricky has been getting his shit together of late. In fact, Ricky and family are just returning in the Shitmobile from a picnic. All rather idyllic—until the radiator explodes, Ray and Lucy pile out of the car yelling at each other, Lahey arrives with fire extinguisher in hand and Ricky whales on Randy. The park thus plunges back into its comfort zone.

"Go mow some lawn or something, you greasy bastard."

Later, Lucy calls Julian. She's had enough of Ricky, they've split. Would he like to come over? Julian, sensing disaster, seeks advice from Bubbles. "Plato's the smartest man that ever lived," Bubbles replies. "He said it's okay to lie if it truly benefits the cause of the people. The cocksucker called it the 'noble lie.' So you have to lie to Lucy, Julian, otherwise she's never going to leave you alone." So Julian tells Lucy that Ricky wants to marry her. Ricky, wasted, bares his soul to Julian about what a fuck-up he is, and how grateful he is for their friendship. They hug, and Cory and Trevor start a rumour that the boys are gay. Julian wastes no time and suggests that some people think Ricky is gay because he's never married Lucy. Ricky is puzzled: "Man, maybe I am gay. Holy fuck, I'm gay!" Julian insists that all Ricky needs to do is get a job and ask Lucy to marry him and all will be cool.

When Levi refuses to yet again set him up with a job, Ricky tries to get a bank loan—only to learn the hard way that aspiring debtors shouldn't tell bankers to go fuck themselves. But one positive comes out of the attempt: Julian picks up a beautiful woman named Candy at the bank.

Desperate, Julian and Ricky break into a jeweller's house to secure a ring for Lucy. They succeed—but not before Ricky is almost killed by a kitten and the kid next door calls 911. During their getaway, a cop pulls them over and Ricky swallows the ring. He then asks the cop if he knows "Jim." Does Ricky mean the officer's father, Jim? A minute later, not only are Ricky and Julian free to go, but Ricky bums two smokes off the cop.

At home, Ricky barfs up the ring, listens to a lecture from Ray on Calvinism and heads to Lucy's trailer. She tells him that Levi got him a job after all, and with this good news he proposes. Despite mixed feelings, Lucy accepts.

Lahey raising shit and Randy with that "pants-off" look in his eyes.

A well-groomed Ricky narrowly avoids becoming gay, thanks to Julian's advice to find a job and get married.

BEST LINES

"Don't you have some offs to fuck there, boys?"
—Ricky to Randy and Lahey

"Tell Mummy I'm sorry. I'm just stressed out because I had to get drunk last night."
—Ricky asking Trinity to make up with Lucy for him

RICKYISMS

"We've got this plutonium kinda love shit going and I don't want to fuck that up, all right? I love you, buddy."
—Ricky telling Julian what a great friend he is

"I haven't drank and drived in over two years!"
—Ricky, pleading with Levi to get him a job

Hey, Ricky, it takes more than a sexy best friend in a tight black T-shirt and impeccably coiffed hair to be gay in the 21st century.

BAD BOYS SCALE

 By Sunnyvale standards, not that boozy. But Ricky does get wasted.

Ricky goes to the bank to get financing for his dope-growing gear—a fact he should have kept to himself, perhaps, when he was talking to the loan officer.

 Ricky takes a few shots at the terrifying kitten that attempts to foil his jewel theft.

Title: WHO THE HELL INVITED THESE IDIOTS TO MY WEDDING ?

Air Date: MAY 27, 2001

Writers: Mike Clattenburg, John Paul Tremblay, Robb Wells, Barrie Dunn
Director: Mike Clattenburg
Guest Stars: James Swansburg, (Officer Ted Johnston), Reverend Bob Chiasson (1st Store Clerk), Ona Archibald (2nd Store Clerk)

The Four Horsemen are one sign of the Apocalypse; another—not mentioned quite so much—is the bit about Ricky: "The end of days will come when Richard begins to not swear so much, only gets drunk on weekends and gets married." Well, if you believe prophecies, you'd better kiss your ass goodbye, because this is precisely what Ricky vows he's going to do. The wedding is on!

The park is abuzz over the biggest event on Sunnyvale's social calendar, but Julian is stressed. Lucy keeps complaining to him about what Ricky has NOT done to prepare for the wedding. Julian assures her everything is okay (even if he has to secretly do the prep work himself). Reassured, Lucy gets back to musing about her upcoming stagette.

"Robberies are simple. It's all about firepower."

Julian and his new girlfriend, Candy, are doing great. Unfortunately, Lucy won't stop hounding him about Ricky. The only way Julian can ensure that the wedding will go off without a hitch is to rob a grocery store to feed the guests. So he organizes a heist—minus Ricky.

Julian's planning would humble the perpetrators of *The Italian Job* or *The Thomas Crown Affair*: 1) Take Ricky to a strip joint and get him so wasted he passes out; 2) Throw him in the back of the truck; 3) Rob a grocery store and load all the shit into shopping carts; 4) Load the carts into the truck and drive like fuck back to the park with the food. Two problems emerge in this otherwise flawless plan: Trevor seems intent on taking most of the Guatemalan banana crop, which really bothers Cory ("Nobody eats bananas at a wedding"), and Ricky wakes up. Oblivious, he staggers into the store for smokes and everyone starts shooting. A bazillion shots later they all realize who they're shooting at, load the truck in a panic and leave. Ricky is furious; he's certainly been caught on camera. Bubbles is pissed about leaving an excellent cart behind.

The next day the wedding goes ahead. Ricky and Lucy exchange beautiful vows—between drags on their respective cigarettes—and manage to get about halfway through the ceremony before the cops arrive and arrest Ricky. Fearing for Ricky's ability to survive in jail alone, Julian says goodbye to Candy and shoots harmlessly into the air to get himself arrested too. Together, the old buddies return to the Van Allen Correctional Centre to end the season.

It's wedding white for Lucy and the classic black tux and handgun for Ricky.

nomesayin

Detective Ted Johnston's brief visit to the trailer park certainly succeeds in intimidating Ricky on his wedding day:

"Yeah, I'm afraid of this cop because he's intense. I'm like a frog running along the highway—eventually some car is going to hit ya and this is the fuckin' car."

Ricky's apprehension is justified, but a frog running along the highway? That's even creepier than the purple squirrels he sees a few seasons later in Sam Losco's veterinary clinic.

rare photo

See you next season.

Looks like there are going to be some empty seats at the wedding reception.

BEST LINES

"A man is coming over to our place tonight to dance with his bum out."
—Trinity commenting on her mom's stagette party

"It's all about the ladies."
—Cory and Trevor commenting on Ricky's stag party

"You're making Bubbles cry, Ricky!"
—Julian asking Ricky to ease off on the verbal abuse after the botched grocery store robbery

Lucy and Ricky's Wedding Vows

"I, Lucy, promise to love you and respect you and be truthful for you. As long as I live."

"I, Richard, promise to love—and to not break the law as much as I used to. I promise to be a good father to my child and to not swear anymore, or as much as I do in public places, and I promise to love you as much as I can and as often as I can under the circumstances."

Groom and best man, looking sharp after their late-night robbery and gunfight.

BAD BOYS SCALE

Ricky gets very wasted the night of his stag—but not drunk enough to keep him from spoiling the robbery.

All quiet on the weed front.

Huge gunfight, while stealing groceries for the wedding reception.

TRAILER PARK BOYS
Postcards from the Park

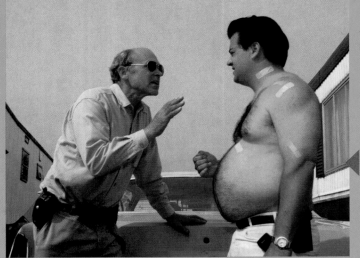

Cirque du Sunnyvale.

Sumo officials won't care if you're not Japanese and you have to take your pants off before you get in the ring.

Sarah could have been a super hero with her much feared "death vision." The only known defence is believed to be Ricktonite.

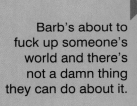

Barb's about to fuck up someone's world and there's not a damn thing they can do about it.

Didn't Nova Scotia fisheries ban drift nets'

SEASON 2

SEASON 2 EPISODE 1

Title: WHAT IN THE FUCK HAPPENED TO OUR TRAILER PARK?

Air Date: JUNE 23, 2002

Writers: Mike Clattenburg, John Paul Tremblay, Robb Wells, Barrie Dun
Director: Mike Clattenburg
Guest Stars: Jarrett Murphy (Soundman), Blain Morris (Terry voice),
Iain MacLeod (Mall Cop), Kim Dunn (Mall Manager)

The boys are out of jail! Bubbles picks them up at the prison gate. Sti
in their wedding clothes, they share the brilliant plan they conceived i
prison: "Freedom 35." They will steal stereos to fund buying dope
growing equipment, grow lots of weed and sell it to prison guards—
who will supply the inmates. Retired by thirty-five. Easy. Bubbles can
help himself: "I picked you up at jail ten minutes ago and now you'r
telling me we're going to steal car stereos." Bubbles wants no part of i
and keeps to his own business when they get to the mall parking lo
stealing shopping carts, rebuilding them and selling them back to
the mall.

"Ricky, what did we agree to in jail?... Julian's thinking is clearer than Ricky's.

A stressed-out mall manager catches Ricky and Julian, but the boy
convince him they are putting stolen stereos back in the cars. They ge
back to the park only to find trash everywhere, cars on fire and Lahe
mired in an alcoholic haze. Besides the mess, Sarah is living with Ra
(she's fallen out with Lucy) and Lucy, well, Lucy is living with Randy
Ricky confronts her with all the wisdom and maturity he gained on th
inside: "You are banging Randy!? THAT is fucked!" The only way to wi
her back is to go straight and get a real job, so he gets a securit
position at the mall.

Ricky begins his employment with a positive outlook: "Basically, it's th
first job I've ever had that's not against the law." These good intention
last about fifty-three seconds, because he has to bust Bubbles fo
stealing carts but can't go through with it. Julian drops by to ask ho
the job is going and witnesses Ricky looking on in agony as one ca
after another is thrown into the ravine by uncaring customers. He ask
Ricky if he's still interested in Freedom 35 and is treated to a
astonishing salvo of fuck-offs and go-fuck-yourselfs. If Julian's going t
salvage their scheme, he has to get Ricky fired.

Using Cory and Trevor to do the dirty work, Julian plants a stole
stereo in the Shitmobile's trunk and alerts the mall manager. Rick
blames Cory and Trevor (who are hauled away), quits his job an
goes back to the park to grow some dope, after Julian cagily admits
"I don't know anything about this fucking hydroponic shit, man. I fee
stupid." Ricky replies, "Now you know how I feel all the time."

Fearless prediction: Ricky won't last a day in this job.

nomesayin

When negotiating with J-Roc over the "re-marketing" of stolen car stereos, be sure to bring a translator along. J-Roc: "As for them car stereos, here's how it's gonna go down, nomesane? I'll get them punk-ass bitches Cory and Trevor roll by your crib once I roll out and get the hydro gear with my mafuckin' crew. Dawg, I wish there was some other shit I could do but the shit's been pimp tight, ya understand?" Translation (courtesy of Bubbles): "He just said Cory and Trevor's going to swing by and drop off the hydro gear and business hasn't been that great."

rare photo
Ray contemplates taking Sarah's bishop, but isn't sure if his beer bottle moves horizontally or diagonally.

We can only pray that the "earthquake" didn't suck up Daisy or Stinkster.

RICKYISM

"Looks like a tropical earthquake blew through here."
—Ricky to Julian, after returning from jail to Sunnyvale

Bubbles isn't too thrilled with Julian and Ricky's Freedom 35 plan. The notion of stealing car stereos the same day you are released from jail seems to be a red flag for trouble.

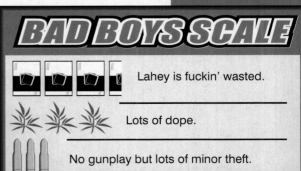

BAD BOYS SCALE

Lahey is fuckin' wasted.

Lots of dope.

No gunplay but lots of minor theft.

SEASON 2 EPISODE 2

Jim looks like he's not quite election-ready.

nomesayin

Anybody notice the Travis Bickle–like character in the crowd during the election debate? You know, the De Niro character from *Taxi Driver* with the mohawk, the army jacket, the shades, a big stinkin' gun under the jacket? He was watching Losco and Lahey pretty closely . . . Losco has enlisted Cory and Trevor to put up signs around the park reading "Jim Lahey Is A Drunk Bastard." Whatever happened to, Ask not what your trailer park can do for you…?

Title: JIM LAHEY IS A DRUNK BASTARD
Air Date: JUNE 30, 2002

Writers: Mike Clattenburg, John Paul Tremblay, Robb Wells, Barrie Dun
Director: Mike Clattenburg
Guest Stars: George Green (Officer George Green), Doug Barron (Channel 10 Reporter)

Julian's worried. Very worried. An election notice announces tha Sunnyvale's resident veterinarian, Sam Losco, will campaign agains incumbent Jim Lahey for the position of trailer park supervisor. A Losc victory would most certainly put a dent in the boys' plans for Freedon 35, as the challenger is promising to be tough on crime. Not good Lahey is a slobbering mess and can't possibly mount a campaign of hi own. Bubbles might not have the sharpest vision, but he reads th situation with 20/20 accuracy: what is afflicting Jim (besides a 40-ounc bottle of booze) is a broken heart. Randy is gone—living with Lucy— and Lahey can't cope without his right-hand man.

"This place looks like the trailer park of the Apocalypse."

Ricky is not particularly sympathetic towards Lahey's emotional stat (okay, he actually doesn't give a fuck), but he's very interested in th state of Lahey's abandoned Airstream trailer: it would be a perfec place to set up the Freedom 35 hydroponic operation. Julian hatche a plan to get Lahey to sign over the lease to the trailer in return fo breaking up Lucy and Randy. (He does this by suggesting to ou shirtless friend that Lucy is only with him in order to make Ricky jealous. He also convinces Jim to run against Losco in the election.

A candidates' debate is staged in the middle of the park and Lahe makes his entrance by crashing his New Yorker through a picke fence. (On a "drunk as fuck" scale, with ten being "really drunk as fuck, Jim scores a twenty.) Things look even bleaker when Losc apprehends the mythical, invulnerable Bottle Kids and hauls them u on the podium to illustrate his dedication to law and order. Nobod has ever caught them before; it's as if Wile E. Coyote caught th Road Runner: such things are not supposed to happen. It looks like crippling blow to Lahey's re-election bid.

But Julian's a regular James Carville behind the Lahey campaign' genteel facade. The boys spike Losco's hot dog with magic mushroom and his election speech begins to sound like something lifted from th pages of *Fear and Loathing in Las Vegas*. (On a "stoned as fuck" scal with ten being "really stoned as fuck," Sam quickly scores a twenty) When Lahey takes the stage, momentum has swung in his favour—an then Randy appears. Lahey's speech elevates to Churchillian levels o intensity, emotion and blood-alcohol percentage. Victory is at hand—a is Randy. "I am Jim Lahey," he concludes commandingly, "and I an your trailer park supervisor."

rare photo

Sam's bid to become Trailer Park Supervisor is almost assured after he captures the infamous Bottle Kids

Jim and Julian engaged in some backroom politics. The fate of Sunnyvale could be at stake.

RICKYISMS

"I can't wait to get this dope operation up and running, boys. I'm telling you, compared to what I had before, this is going to be way, way, way awesomer!"
—Ricky in the new Airstream dope trailer

"What are your thoughts on the incumbent?"
—TV reporter's question to Ricky.

"On the what?" —Ricky's reply

"The incumbent."

"What are you doing using your big school words? Why don't you just use normal people words and I'll understand what you're talking about?"

Sam's inability to speak coherently begins to "mushroom" during his failed campaign speech.

BAD BOYS SCALE

Lahey WASTED!

Weed growing and mushrooms.

Not really. Just a little drinkin' and drivin'.

SEASON 2 EPISODE 3

Title: I'VE MET CATS AND DOGS SMARTER THAN TREVOR AND CORY

Air Date: JULY 7, 2002

Writers: Mike Clattenburg, John Paul Tremblay, Robb Wells, Barrie Dunn
Director: Mike Clattenburg
Guest Stars: George Green (Police Officer), Robert Klingerman (Kitten),

The prison guards are calling non-stop looking for their dope orders and Ricky doesn't know if Freedom 35 has the infrastructure (although he would never use such a word) to meet the demand. Julian, of course, has a plan. If the boys open a nightclub in the park, they can use the profits to buy more equipment and grow way more weed. He enlists Cory and Trevor to rob a warehouse for the gear needed to open the new nightspot, JROCS CRIB "LICENSED."

"Do you guys got any jimmy hats?"

Meanwhile, Randy's birthday BBQ is underway. The boys drop by to divert Lahey's attention from the truckload of stolen gear about to enter the park. But Cory and Trevor return empty-handed, and baked out of their minds. It seems they never found the place they were supposed to rob. Trevor was certainly eager—"We can't fuck this up Cory"—but then he sparked a joint, and the next thing to come out of his mouth was "Shit, what was I talking about?" Julian sends them back out for the gear, with a bitching and moaning Ricky along to supervise the heist—which will soon prove deserving of an entire wing in the Inept Robberies Hall of Fame. Alarms go off, guard dogs charge, and Ricky manages to shoot himself in the foot. But they do escape with the gear.

The boys set up the nightclub and it's soon packed. Ah, the money is about to start rolling in. One wrinkle presents itself, however. As Bubbles relates: "I think Julian was the first one to notice, but I knew something weird was up. It was all guys in there; nice clothes, nice cologne, and Sarah was the only girl there." Julian asks Cory and Trevor where they put up flyers in town. In a bar called the Empty Closet, they reply. Julian restrains his temper, but neglects to tell Cory and Trevor that the two women they are hitting on are transvestites.

Randy soon arrives and busts up the party, but not without striking a deal with Julian: if the boys let him shut down the party, he won't involve the cops. This way the boys can keep all the profits while Randy, who is soloing as weekend park supervisor for the first time, looks good to Lahey. Julian agrees.

The show winds up with Cory and Trevor, arm in arm with the "ladies," asking the boys if they can spare any "jimmy hats."

Cory can't wait to get with the "ladies" from the Empty Closet bar. Trevor senses something might be up.

nomesayin

For the first time we meet Jim Lahey's daughter, Treena, an obviously intelligent, well-adjusted preteen. She really likes all the people her dad has warned her about, and happily runs errands for Ricky, buying him chicken chips and pepperoni.

If you are going to rob a warehouse, and your name is Ricky, make sure you leave Cory and Trevor at home; and while you're at it leave your gun at home, too. If Cory and Trevor must accompany you and you have no option but to shoot yourself in the foot, do not wrap your bleeding toes with Trevor's disgusting T-shirt. The vet would never approve.

rare photo

JROCS CRIB is Sunnyvale's hottest night spot. It's so hot, it's flaming.

You won't find a cat or dog who can work a pair of bolt cutters better than Trevor and Cory.

RICKYISM

"Julian gets an order for twice as much more dope and he thinks he can just wave some money around and the magical fairy grandmother of dope is going to come and . . . give us twice as much dope. That's not gonna happen."
—Ricky on supply issues in the narcotics industry

Cory and Trevor haven't fucked up this heist yet. But the night is young.

BAD BOYS SCALE

Nothing excessive by park standards, though J-Roc's club unlikely to have a licence.

All of this was orchestrated in order to buy more equipment to grow more dope.

Although there wasn't a lot of gunplay, there was enough to get Ricky shot with his own bullet. Ouch!

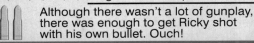

Bubbles dreams of a better life for his kitties than guarding dope plants.

nomesayin

MR. LAHEY'S SHIT ANALOGIES

"He's about to enter the shit tornado to Oz."

TRAILER PARK UNIVERSITY

Pygocentrus nattereri
Piranhas, or pirañas, are carnivorous fish normally found only in the freshwater river systems of South America. Their sharp teeth, aggression and astonishing appetite for flesh have made the fish notorious. The word "piranha" is sometimes pronounced piranagus by Ricky, and is often used to describe "little dope-eating insects."

Title: A DOPE TRAILER IS NO PLACE FOR A KITTY
Air Date: JULY 14, 2002

Writers: Mike Clattenburg, John Paul Tremblay, Robb Wells, Barrie Dunn
Director: Mike Clattenburg
Guest Stars: Joanne Hagen (Librarian)

"Here kitty, kitty, kitty." We find Bubbles in a reflective mood as he introduces his most treasured possessions, while looking for one of his many cats. His beautifully appointed shed features a vintage 1961 Electro Bubble bubble-maker. This appliance (and in Bubbles's world, it is most certainly an appliance) is the only memento he has from his parents, who disappeared long ago. Not only does the machine have tremendous sentimental value, it also amuses the shit out of his cats: "Every kitty I ever met loves these things." This peaceful interlude is ruined when the Shitmobile comes sliding to a stop in front of his shed—crashing into a few shopping carts along the way. Ricky emerges, carrying an ailing cat swaddled in a blanket; he's concerned that without Bubbles's "guard cats" the squirrels will ruin the Freedom 35 crop, so he's come for reinforcements. Exasperated, Bubbles insists that "A dope trailer is no place for a kitty."

"It's not a hard job for a cat to keep the fuckin' squirrels away from your plants."

The dope-growing operation is going well, until Ricky notices the plants aren't thriving. He expertly diagnoses the problem: "Dope-eating insects. They're gonna wipe out the whole fuckin' crop!" To make matters worse, Lahey has caught wind of the boys' operation and is threatening to call the cops. And to make matters worser, as Ricky might say, Sam Losco, for reasons unknown, is scattering half-eaten hot dogs all about the park and suggesting that Bubbles's cats have rabies.

Treena suggests that the boys get a book on horticulture to help with the infestation and hooks Ricky up with his first library card. They find a book about "horviculture," which identifies the problem as a spider-mite infestation. If they "quantrateen" the plants, Ricky learns, and introduce mite-eating ladybugs, the dope should thrive once again. Ricky and Julian decide to move all the weed into Bubbles's home (without his knowledge) to hide it from Lahey and the cops. Ricky and Trevor rewire the shed for additional electricity—promptly burning it down. Bubs is devastated—particularly over the loss of his bubble-maker—and takes his rage out on Losco with a set of nunchuks. Fortunately, Julian intervenes before anyone is mortally wounded, or even really hurt, and insists that Sam stop scattering hot dogs around the park because they are making Bubbles's cats sick.

In the end, the park rallies around Bubbles: Ricky apologizes, J-Roc rents him his van to live in at a reasonable rate and Treena (God bless her) presents him with a miniature bubble-maker.

rare photo
Treena saves the day, and the dope plants, by suggesting the boys can solve their bug problem by going to the library.

Bubbles decides to leave the helmet on for this intense Ricky scolding.

RICKYISM

"It's a Catch-23 situation because I got something fuckin' around with my dope plants."
—Ricky explains his horvicultural quandary

Bubbles loses his shed and bubble-maker but not his will to make the best of a bad situation.

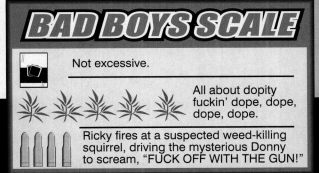

BAD BOYS SCALE

Not excessive.

All about dopity fuckin' dope, dope, dope, dope.

Ricky fires at a suspected weed-killing squirrel, driving the mysterious Donny to scream, "FUCK OFF WITH THE GUN!"

Title: THE BIBLE PIMP
Air Date: JULY 21, 2002

Writers: Mike Clattenburg, John Paul Tremblay, Robb Wells, Barrie Dunn
Director: Mike Clattenburg
Guest Stars: George Green (Police Officer), Brian Green II (Second Police Officer), Jacob Rolfe (Jacob), Tania Rudolph (Tanya)

Looking up from his conversation with his kitty Daisy, Bubbles watches a father and daughter bible-selling team approach. Introducing themselves as Hampton and Tanya, they explain to an immediately skeptical Bubbles that they are spreading the good news of the Lord. Something doesn't feel right to Bubbles, and when the pair question his literacy skills he dismisses them with what may very well be the finest comeback ever. Truth be told, Bubbles has been in a foul mood since the boys burned down his shed. Julian's attempt at apology—a huge jar of pickled eggs—is swiftly, if not wholeheartedly, rejected. Across the park in the Airstream dope trailer, Ricky apologizes to Lucy for neglecting her. He's facing a huge workload, trying to finally get his grade ten and producing a gargantuan weed crop. It's a busy time. Later, Julian agrees to watch the dope trailer while Ricky takes Sarah out for Chinese food, but Julian is himself quickly distracted by the beautiful Tanya (who doesn't quite believe Julian is a hemp farmer and rope maker). The only other person that doesn't seem wary of these two is Ray, who buys Ricky a bible.

"Don't pay any attention. You're beautiful, Randy."

Bubbles puts aside his anger and tries to convince Julian that something is not right with this pair. Julian ignores him; he would do well to take his own advice—think, Julian, think!—but he takes Tanya out to dinner and leaves the trailer unguarded.

Ricky and Julian, and their respective dates, meet at the Chinese drive-in and an argument breaks out over who's neglecting the dope. Julian returns to the park to find that Tanya has clearly conned him: the pot is gone—along, it seems, with Freedom 35. Bubbles, however, had Cory and Trevor tail Hampton and knows where the pot is. He also delivers a heartfelt speech that roughly translates as follows: You stand by your friends, even when they behave like dicks by burning down your home and then forget your egg rolls (Ricky!).

The entire crew heads down to the Slick Pimp strip joint and finds Tanya dancing on stage in a red bra and matching knickers, with Hampton hooting in the audience. A Starsky and Hutch-like chase/shootout ensues in the parking lot. The cops soon arrive in response to the gunfire and arrest the "bible pimps." "Ah, don't worry about her, Julian," Bubbles consoles, his eyes getting even bigger as he watches the cops throw Tanya into the cruiser. "Jesus Christ, she is hot, though!" The boys recover their dope and, once home, apologize properly to Bubbles. Ricky and Julian even allow Cory and Trevor rare brotherly handshakes. Not a dry eye in the house.

Nobody wants to listen to Bubbles. Fuck, they even forgot his Chinese takeout.

nomesayin

Bible salesman Hampton refers to Lahey alternately as "Commander" and "Lieutenant."

Ricky is made to write lines on the school blackboard à la Bart Simpson: "I will not swear in class."

Ray responds to Hampton's questioning of Bubbles's sanity/intelligence with "Bubbles? Are you crazy? He's the sharpest guy in the park." Truer words were never spoken.

rare photo

A hard-working hemp farmer takes a well-deserved break.

Rare surveillance photo of bible pimps, Hampton and Tanya.

BEST LINES

"Have you read the Bible?"
—Tanya asking Bubbles

"Can you read, my son?"
—Hampton asking Bubbles

"Well, that depends. Can you go fuck yourselves?"
—Bubbles replying to Hampton and Tanya

"And don't think you can buy me off with a jar of those delicious things."
—Bubbles, pointing to the jar of pickled eggs proffered by Julian

"I can't believe I got in a shoot-out and didn't get shot."
—Ricky to Julian

RICKY and GRADE 10

"Grade ten, it's got me all stressed out. It's way fuckin' harder than grade nine. Way fuckin' harder!"
—Ricky complaining to Julian

"Holy fuck it's hard. I've got to learn these new math equations and new languages and shit. The only fucking course that isn't too bad is gym. I scored twelve goals in floor hockey."
—Ricky telling Sarah about school

The boys had to do some serious apologizing to get back in Bubbles's good books. Even more serious than pickled eggs.

BAD BOYS SCALE

Not much to speak of.

Freedom 35 . . . it's all about the weed.

Huge shootout at the end of the episode, as well as the criminal, sinful sauciness of the bible salesbabe, Tanya.

Title: NEVER TRUST A MAN WITH NO SHIRT ON
Air Date: JULY 28, 2002

Writers: Mike Clattenburg, John Paul Tremblay, Robb Wells, Barrie Dunn
Director: Mike Clattenburg
Guest Stars: George Green (Officer George Green), Brian Green II (Second Police Officer)

Growing weed on a large scale demands a great deal of electricity. In Sunnyvale that kind of power is right there for the taking—provided you're willing to climb up a splinter-filled hydro pole to poke around a 200-bazillawatt transformer in the dark and answer to the name of "Ricky." Not surprisingly, the challenge doesn't worry him: "I've been stealing power since fuckin' grade seven. I know what I'm fuckin' doing here." Unfortunately, Lahey also knows what Ricky's doing—and Lahey's determined to send him back to con college.

"See boys, a fake-piss apparatus. Never trust a man with no shirt on."

The tension is not just in the wires: Ricky electrocutes himself, burns his shirt and gets into a huge fight (that Treena overhears) with Julian over money. It's plain to see, Ricky's self-esteem has been taking a beating lately (no grade ten, lives in a car, clothes are shitty, etc., etc.). Treena does her best to cheer him up, saying, "Ricky, you are smart." Meanwhile, Lahey enlists the help of an electrician, who, looking at the remnants of a charred cable, comments, "Whoever did this is really stupid. You're dealing with a dangerous moron."

An increasingly nasty-tempered Lahey is furious with Treena for hanging around the boys. He's also drinking more, and during a frustrating confrontation with Ricky and Julian he calls Randy a "disobedient, fat bastard"—ouch!—and fires him. So Randy throws his lot in with the boys and soon becomes their gopher—sent on runs for rum and chips. As the ultimate test of Randy's new loyalty, Julian, who isn't buying Randy's conversion, insists that he piss on Lahey's New Yorker. Randy happily obliges.

Jim calls in the cops following a thorough surveillance, and the boys relocate their plants to Ray's trailer. While doing so, they discover that Randy is wearing a wire, and a fake-piss apparatus. Realizing Lahey is one step ahead of them, Julian and Co. put a little quick thinking and some power tools to good use, and rearrange all the street names and trailer numbers. When the police arrive their search warrant is useless.

Things wrap up with Ricky sombrely telling Treena that she should stay away from him and the boys for a while because of their "activities." Disappointed, but understanding, she tells Ricky to kick butt in his upcoming grade ten exams. Later on, with Julian holding a continent-sized chunk of hash, the boys toast Freedom 35.

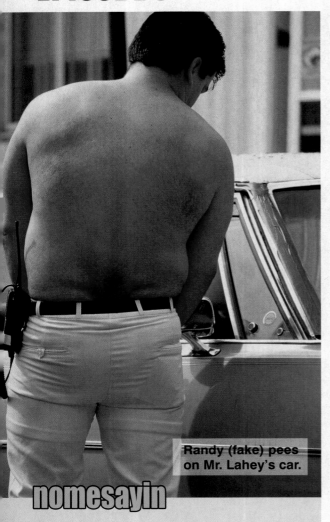

Randy (fake) pees on Mr. Lahey's car.

nomesayin

MR. LAHEY'S SHIT ANALOGIES

"Dope and cops don't mix, do they, Mr. Lahey?"
"Like shit and strawberry shortcake, Randy."

"You know what a shit rope is Julian? It's a rope covered in shit that criminals try to hold on to. You see, the shit kind of acts like grease. The harder you try to climb up, the tighter you try to hold on, the faster you slide down the rope, Julian. All the way to jail."—Lahey to the boys, as they await the arrival of the police

"I'm afraid of shit rope, boys . . . what's a shit rope?"—Bubbles expressing the sort of anxiety he usually reserves for samsquanches

rare photo
The boys are once again one step ahead of the cops —switching trailer numbers this time.

Shifty and shirtless Randy's undercover plans are exposed.

"Just pretend you're a squirrel, Ricky."
—Bubbles looking up at Ricky as he climbs a hydro pole

"Why don't you pretend you're somebody fucking off."
—Ricky

"What's the capital city of British Columbia?"
—Treena asking a simple question to make Ricky feel better about himself

"Victoriaville."
—Ricky, with hockey on the brain.

"Make like a tree and fuck off."
—Ricky

RICKYISMS

"Jalapeño, what flavour's that?"
—Ricky to Julian

"Ricky, the J's silent. You're saying it wrong."
—Julian

"The J's like an H, Ricky. HALAPEENO. Not julapanoh."
—Bubbles

"What in the fuck are you guys talking about?"
—Ricky

"HALAPEENO. That's how you pronounce it."
—Bubbles

"I know how to pronounce it. I ordered fuckin' julapanoh."
—Ricky to Bubs

Lahey doesn't want Treena hanging around Ricky. Something about him being a bad influence.

BAD BOYS SCALE

 Rum supplied to the boys by Randy as a peace offering.

Ricky bypassing the meter so he can grow dope and almost getting electrocuted.

 Cory and Trevor take Treena's bike in a pawn arrangement so she can buy pepperoni and a shirt for Ricky.

Title: THE BARE PIMP PROJECT
Air Date: AUGUST 4, 2002

Writers: Mike Clattenburg, John Paul Tremblay, Robb Wells, Barrie Dunn
Director: Mike Clattenburg
Guest Stars: George Green (Police Officer), Bernard Robichaud (Cyrus), Annemarie Cassidy (Other Police Officer), Lara Cassidy (Witch #1), Shaun R Clarke (Prison Guard), Brian Green II (2nd Police Officer), Nicole McLean (Witch #2), Celia Alida Rutte (Witch #3), Michael Volpe (Gas Station Attendant)

It's the busy end of another season, but nothing is more important than Ricky's grade ten exams! Fittingly, he's doing bottle tokes in the dope trailer. Julian enters, sees his condition—and the new weed clones sprouting at his side—and is furious: "No more breaking the law!" They'll sell the hash they already have to the guards and retire. "Freedom 35, remember? No more jail," says Julian. "It's like asking N.W.A to stop being black," Ricky replies. "I grow fuckin' dope!"

Julian is also worried that Sam Losco is about to marry Barb Lahey—Jim's ex and the owner of Sunnyvale. If this happens, life could get complicated for the boys. Julian approaches J-Roc to direct another film of an adult nature—one starring Sam. A video like that would end Barb's engagement to (as J-Roc puts it) "the greasy hot-dog eatin' neanderthal muthafucka." J-Roc agrees and they convince Sam to star in *The Bare Pimp Project*—an art-house erotic film that is light on the art, and even lighter on the erotic. Ever frisky, Bubbles once again is eager to assume his acting duties.

"I'm not going to run over a kitty to save your dope, Ricky!"

More cerebral things are going on in class, as Ricky sits for his exams. But he's distracted by the presence of Cyrus (guess who else never got his grade ten?), who tells on Ricky for smoking at his desk. Ricky replies in kind and tells the teacher Cyrus is cheating. She dismisses Cyrus and Ricky adds, "Have fun getting a job since you're kicked out of grade ten—ya dummy." Good to see Ricky finally taking book learnin' seriously.

Julian delivers the hash to the prison guards and the finished *Bare Pimp Project* to Barb, ending the engagement. Things look good, but like the Perfect Sunnyvale Shitstorm, Cyrus, Losco, Lahey and the cops all descend upon Ricky and Julian for payback. A spectacular gunfight ensues and the boys get away—Bubbles driving Lahey's truck, towing the Airstream dope trailer behind them. An O.J. Simpson-inspired chase follows, until Bubbles swerves to avoid hitting a kitty. The truck rolls and the trailer bursts into flame. The boys scramble out (Julian's drink still intact), but Ricky is devastated. He thinks he's watching Freedom 35 go up in smoke, until Julian tells him that he already sold the dope. Bubbles avoids jail time by pretending to be a farmer. Ricky and Julian are busted, but Bubbles and Treena hide the cash for when the boys get out of jail. The season ends behind bars, with Ricky proudly announcing that he passed his grade ten. You're an inspiration to us all, Ricky.

"Pretend you know me."

nomesayin

Michael Volpe, one of the show's producers, delivers a breathtaking performance in this episode with his nuanced portrayal of a gas station attendant. He pumps $2.37 worth of gas into the Shitmobile (Ricky only asked for $2.35 worth).

rare photo

Bubbles is left to celebrate Ricky's graduation alone. The boys are back in jail.

Bubbles in the starring role—half fearful, half frisky.

RICKYISM

'Do you people want me to fail grade ten? I've got all this dope stuff and Lucy and Cyrus on my mind—and you fuckin' idiots following me around. I can't handle this, guys. But you make my words, I'm going to get my grade ten and everybody else can catch a boat to Fuckoffy Land."

—Ricky heading into his exam after finding out Lucy is banging Cyrus

Barb gets in Sam's face about his appearance in J-Roc's porn video.

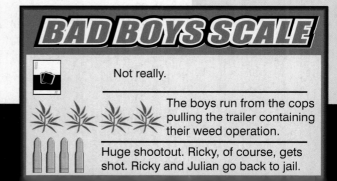

BAD BOYS SCALE

Not really.

The boys run from the cops pulling the trailer containing their weed operation.

Huge shootout. Ricky, of course, gets shot. Ricky and Julian go back to jail.

TRAILER PARK BOYS
Postcards from the Park

Ricky creates a life-like replica of his own head to trick the guards while he escapes from jail. Wait...no...that's his actual head. Hmmm...he isn't that cunning anyway.

Cory and Trevor waiting for their next command.

Is Jim seeing Randy on the side?

Nothing but the thin strands of chain link stand between Sunnyvale and a place called Allhellbrokeloose.

"You boys were standing in a "No Belly Zone." I'm gonna have to write you up."

SEASON 3

Title: KISS OF FREEDOM
Air Date: APRIL 20, 2003

Writers: Mike Clattenburg, John Paul Tremblay, Robb Wells, Jackie Torrens
Director: Mike Clattenburg
Guest Stars: Brian Heighton (Lawyer), Mauralea Austin (Saleswoman)

Bubbles opens the show convinced that this is one of the "best day ever." Not only has he scored four excellent shopping carts t "re-market," but he's on his way to pick up Ricky and Julian, who ge out of jail (again) today. But this time they'll be flush, with $35,000 i unmarked bills waiting for them, safely hidden by Bubbles and Treena

However, upon their return, a philosophical conflict arises betwee Ricky and Julian: Julian wants to invest the cash in small-scal business around the park (and avoid another trip to jail); Ricky, on th other hand, would like to buy a trailer from Mr. Lahey, then blow th rest of his money on getting wasted. They decide to split their mone and go their separate ways. Lahey, certain Ricky could never come u with the cash, and reluctant to allow Ricky to stake a permanent clain in the park, will accept nothing less than a $5,000 deposit by the en of the day—or no trailer. Offended by this demand, Ricky says that he doesn't have the money by Lahey's deadline, he will get down o his knees and, in front of the whole park, kiss Lahey's ass.

"Holy fuck, that's good pepperoni."

For the remainder of the day, Ricky and Julian compete to win th favour of Bubbles and the others by purchasing lavish gifts: Julia outfits Bubbles with a new shed (with bunk beds, the world's large: cellphone and an indoor toilet: "This is the nicest fuckin' shed I thin there's ever been," says Bubs). Not to be outdone, Ricky buys hir a go-kart. Things continue to sour between Julian and Ricky, an eventually come to a head with Ricky blasting away at Julian's ne ice-cream carts—piloted, of course, by Cory and Trevor. Ricky's plan for trailer ownership come crashing down around him following spending orgy of Caligulan proportions. He nearly exhausts his ha of the hash money and is forced to choose between purchasing $4,700 set of encyclopedias he'd ordered for his daughter, Trinity, o making the down payment on the trailer. To prove he's a good fathe Ricky opts for the encyclopedias. Much to his own, and Randy' disgust ("Make it a quick one, Ricky!"), he kisses Lahey's bare ass o bended knee.

But Ricky's pucker does not go unappreciated, and he wins th respect of the witnesses and a heartfelt gift of pepperoni from h daughter. Best tasting pepperoni ever.

Trevor rides tall aboard one of Julian's legit ice-cream carts.

nomesayin

Bubbles's tabby cat has its face blurred out the entire episode and Bubbles's hoists a massive vintage cellphone.

MR. LAHEY'S SHIT ANALOGIES

"I don't trust you, shit-bat."—Lahey to Ricky, regarding the trailer deposit

"The old shit clock's tickin'."

rare photo

The fleet sets to sale, Captains Cory and Trevor at the helm.

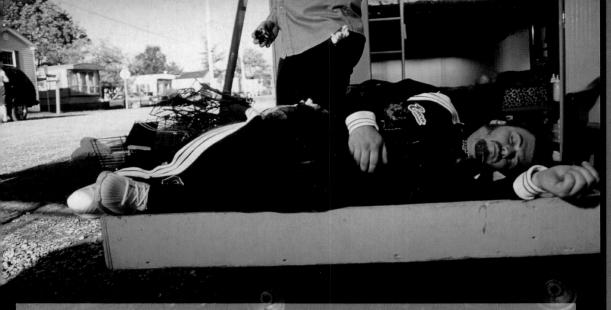

"I plan on getting drunk as fuck!" Ricky recovers from a whole day of way too much freedom while involuntarily testing the towing capacity of Bubbles's new go-kart.

RICKYISM

"Fuck RRPPs Julian."

TRAILER PARK TIPS

If there was ever an argument needed to convince today's youth of the importance of staying in school and paying attention to book learning, watching Ricky kiss Lahey's ass is it. If Ricky had been born with just a little more brains (okay, a lot more brains) and if he had stuck with school, he probably would never have been humiliated in the business world by having to kiss his superior's ass. In the corporate environment, ass kissing is usually a figurative activity and only occasionally literal. Stay in school kids!

◀ Ricky arrives with Bubbles's new ride.

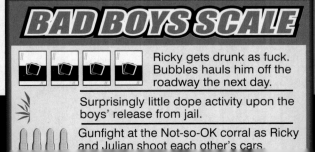

SEASON 3
EPISODE 2

Title: TEMPORARY RELIEF ASSISTANT TRAILER PARK SUPERVISOR

Air Date: APRIL 27, 2003

Writers: Mike Clattenburg, John Paul Tremblay, Robb Wells, Jackie Torrens, Michael Volpe
Director: Mike Clattenburg
Guest Stars: George Green (Officer George Green), Jacob Rolfe (Jaco

Sunnyvale is in disarray this morning. Mr. Lahey is doing his best to rescue Bubbles's cat Sergeant Meowenstein, who is stuck down a well—it seems Randy neglected to put the cover back on. Barb i none too happy with Randy's negligence, and in a display of authority suspends him for three weeks. This leaves the park minus one assistant trailer park supervisor, so Lahey advertises the temporary position to the other residents. This couldn't come at a better time for Ricky, who is in desperate need of cash (when is Ricky not in need of cash?), and he applies for the gig.

"I'd lend you money, Ricky, but fuck, I've go twenty-eight cats to look after in this park."

After serious competition from Cory, Trevor and Bubbles (well, the "serious competition" comes only from Bubbles—Cory and Trevo are, after all, idiots), Ricky wins the job by demonstrating hi proficiency in gathering recycling waste (Lahey judges success b weight) when he successfully bags an entire tailpipe. Reluctantly Lahey gives Ricky the job, but makes it very clear he will d everything—within the rules—to get him fired. Ricky is now working for the enemy. Meanwhile, Julian has become a full-time bootlegge and has employed Cory and Trevor to sell illicit Russian vodka around the park out of backpacks. Clearly, this state of affairs i going to further strain the boys' relationship, especially when the power of being assistant trailer park supervisor goes straight to Ricky's head.

Ricky—driving Mr. Lahey's New Yorker—goes so far as to pull ove Bubbles in his go-kart. ("Ricky, when did you become such an asshole?") If that isn't a violation of friendship, what is? It's only a matter of time before Lahey catches wind of Julian's vodka-running scheme—from Ricky—and calls in the big guns. Anticipating tha Lahey will call the cops, Julian empties all the vodka into a wading pool, where he figures no one will ever think to look for it—a cleve plan, except that Ricky and Randy decide that beating each othe senseless in the middle of this oasis is a good idea. The booze reservoir is dumped, Ricky is promptly fired ("You can't fire me 'cause I already quit"), Julian's bootlegging plans are dashed Bubbles could see it all coming and everything is once again righ in Sunnyvale.

Ricky's walking tall— actually leaning tall— in his new uniform.

nomesayin

Ricky squeezes vodka out of his drenched ka-hay-ki trailer park assistant shirt in order to make a screwdriver.

MR. LAHEY'S SHIT ANALOGIES

"Why bother with two stupid shit sticks when you can have the whole shit trawler?"—Ricky to Lahey, after catching Cory and Trevor selling Julian's booze
"Nice shit analogy, Ricky."—Lahey

rare photo

Bubbles about to be pulled over and ticketed by the new Assistant Trailer Park Supervisor

Why, there's enough vodka to fill a small swimming pool.

RICKYISMS

"How to get stains out of ka-hay-ki pants?"
—Ricky reading from the assistant trailer park supervisor job-application questionnaire

"Ricky, if you are serious about applying for this job, you be here tomorrow for an aptitude test."
—Lahey

"What's an aptitude test?"
—Ricky

"Suitability test, Ricky."

"I'll wear a suit if I have to."

Sergeant Meowenstein is happily reunited with his family following a daring rescue from a well. Seems that Randy fucked up and left the cover off, endangering the lives of all of Sunnyvale's four-legged, furry little residents.

BAD BOYS SCALE

A wading pool full of illicit vodka and door-to-door liquor sales jack up the booze meter here.

Smoke-free episode.

No gunfire, but Julian's huge bootlegging scheme goes down the drain.

93

SEASON 3 EPISODE 3

The siphoning life . . .
A hard, lonely road
indeed.

nomesayin

If you listen carefully to Ricky during this episode, you can learn a fantastic amount about how the global oil business operates: "I have to steal gas 'cause I'm broke and gas is a fortune now because of all the government bullshit taxes and stuff. It pisses me off because in provinces like Texas and Calgary it's not so bad. It should be the same everywhere." Ricky can also teach us all a lot about the actual chemistry of gasoline. When Trevor asks Ricky how to determine which type of fuel is which, while siphoning, Ricky responds: "What, are you fuckin' stupid? Unleaded tastes tangy, supreme is kinda sour and diesel tastes pretty good."

MR. LAHEY'S SHIT ANALOGIES

"We are about to sail into a shit typhoon so you better haul in the jib before it gets covered in shit."

Title: IF I CAN'T SMOKE AND SWEAR I'M FUCKED
Air Date: MAY 4, 2003

Writers: Mike Clattenburg, John Paul Tremblay, Robb Wells, Jackie Torrens
Director: Mike Clattenburg
Guest Stars: Jennifer Overton (Judge), Jeremy Akerman (Prosecutor)

A fan favourite, this episode features Cory and Trevor getting really fucked up siphoning gas and Ricky telling just about everybody to fuck off. It also contains a touching father-daughter moment when, out of paternal concern, Ricky confronts nine-year-old Trinity about her smoking habit and subsequent nicotine patch addiction. The fun starts when Julian tells the boys that they are still going to break the law to make their fortune, but from now on they are going to do so at a much lower level, to avoid the unwanted attention of Mr. Lahey and the police. As an incentive, he promises everybody who buys into his plan a cruise ship vacation at the end of the year. To pay for this trip, they open an illegal gas station, one based on a business model that takes advantage of very low supplier costs—specifically, they siphon gas from cars and resell it at a cut-rate price in the park.

"The defence rests. Everybody else can fuck off."

An elaborate sales operation evolves, with Lucy and Sarah acting as middlewomen by selling gas coupons through their hairdressing business—although Mr. Lahey is convinced the girls are running a prostitution ring out of their trailer. A sting is in order. Randy and Lahey make an appointment with the ladies, but find themselves treated to nothing less than the hottest hairstyling either of them has ever had. Realizing that gasoline and not flesh is what's up for sale in Sunnyvale, they set to planning a second sting operation.

This time, Randy cleverly goes undercover looking for some cheap gas. A poorly hidden camera records the transaction, and the boys clearly implicate Cory and Trevor on video just as the police arrive. Yet that doesn't prevent the police from charging the entire crew and hauling them all into court. Facing jail so soon after tasting the fruits of freedom, Ricky turns over his defence to the only person he can truly trust to get him out of a jam with the law: himself. And he conducts himself brilliantly, but only after the judge allows him to smoke and swear in court. Some say it will be Ricky's finest hour. He successfully gets everybody cleared of charges—except Cory and Trevor, of course, who take the fall for the entire operation. Once again, all is right with the world.

rare photo

Even siphoned gas is flammable.

Ricky saves the Shitmobile by throwing himself between it and the flames.

"Jail is fun and food is really good in there."
—Ricky

"Trinity has got to quit smokin'. I can't have her smokin' anymore, it's ridiculous."
—Ricky worrying about his preteen daughter's habit

RICKYISMS

"He's distraculating me from my case."
—Ricky, pointing to the prosecuting attorney in court

"I'd like to make a request under the People's Freedom of Choices and Voices Act."
—Ricky's misguided yet successful legal motion in court

◄ The old-time feel of a full-service gas station is captured when the boys open a discount gas business in Sunnyvale.

BAD BOYS SCALE

Julian rummages for bottle dregs to fill his glass.	
	Cory and Trevor are rewarded with joints for not ratting out the boys.
	Trinity drops Ricky's gun in a variety store and it fires. The clerk thinks it's a robbery. Ricky steals some stuff to make it seem right. Plus stealing gas, then reselling it.

J-Roc layin' it down hard. Sunnyvale style!

nomesayin

J-Roc's CD is called J-Roc and Friendz.

Rapper DVS makes his Sunnyvale debut. DVS stands for Detroit Velvet Smooth, even though DVS is from Moncton.

The back of Ray's wheelchair says, "Please return to lobby."

Title: WHO'S THE MICROPHONE ASSASSIN?
Air Date: MAY 11, 2003

Writers: Mike Clattenburg, John Paul Tremblay, Robb Wells, Jackie Torrens
 Director: Mike Clattenburg
 Guest Stars: Linda Busby (J-Roc's Mom)

Arguably, "Who's the Microphone Assassin," with J-Roc in the spotlight, is one of the series' pivotal episodes; expect to see it used as a teaching tool in Canadian university sociology courses for years to come. It explores Canada's racial divide with power, grace and sensitivity—and, more importantly, this is the episode in which J-Roc gets caught by his mom and the boys masturbating in his bedroom. "He's pulling his goalie!" observes Bubbles.

The events that lead up to this seminal moment centre around Julian and the boys successfully marketing J-Roc's CD (not "CB," Ricky) at the Sunnyvale flea market. After turning a tidy profit, Julian conceives of a plan to become the Suge Knight of Sunnyvale and promote a rap concert with J-Roc as the headline act. Ricky's plan to serve free Jiffy Wine virtually guarantees success. But the event almost falls apart after J-Roc is caught "gettin' changed, muthafucka" ("jerking off," for those of you not from Compton) and his self-confidence takes a beating. With a great deal of encouragement, Julian—a master ego stroker if there ever was one—convinces him to go ahead with the show as planned.

"He's pullin' his goalie."

Mr. Lahey, bent on shutting down the event and dispersing the crowd, informs Detroit Velvet Smooth—a rapper from New Brunswick, not Michigan, who is liberally sampled in J-Roc's recordings—that he is being ripped off. DVS duly arrives at the park, out for blood. He confronts J-Roc mid-concert, weapon in hand, and humiliates him. His accusation that J-Roc is rather light in the being black department is particularly devastating. In disgrace, our hero retreats into his bedroom and once again assumes the identity he so loathes: that of a twenty-nine-year-old white kid living in his mom's trailer. The show is now in peril, so Julian enlists Bubbles to stand in for J-Roc. He may have never rapped before, but Bubbles delivers some hard and fast kitty rhymes that win the crowd back. Meanwhile, after much persuasion from Julian and J-Roc's mom, plus a toke or three, DVS sees the error of his hasty judgment and restores J-Roc's blackness. The concert delivers as promised, with J-Roc and DVS taking the stage together while Jiffy Wine flows as freely as the rhymes. Once again, all is well in Sunnyvale. Peace out.

rare photo
Rappers "Prime Minister" and "T-Bag."

By now you've heard the story of how I got caught,
playing with my shit, but hold that thought.
Before you disrespect J-R-O-C,
it could happen to you, 'cuz it happened to me.
The situation broke out when I smoked too much bud,
reached in my drawers, pulled out my pud.
Bust open a jar of petroleum jelly,
started thinkin' 'bout Donna, Nicky and Shelly.
[muttering] I was hittin' that we was almost there,
then the door bust open and fuck my maz was there.
Before you disrespect J-R-O-C,
it could happen to you, 'cuz it happened to me.

The Microphone Assassin and DVS (Detroit Velvet Smooth): awkward first meeting. DVS later tells J-Roc his "shit is tight."

Bubbles's Rap

Got a grey kitty, white one and a tabby too,
and a big orange cat who puts snakes
in my shoes.
Mad MC skills ...[muttering]
And I roll with my kitties and I'm hard as fuck.
I'm down with Plato and Socrates,
and I like to get busy with all the lay-dees.
[muttering] Something, something, something
something, (groan, groan) get
enough of my shit up in my shed.

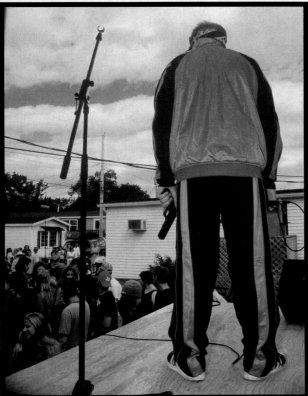

"So I was just getting myself in a sex vibe and some mafuckas bust in and misinterpret it thinking I was yanking my shit but that ain't even true, nomesayin. Straight up, writing some shit of a sexual place, of a sexual nature, right, that's some of the rhymes right there, nomesayin, and I couldn't of written that 'less I had my shit out, right, and some hand cream."

BEST LINES

"You idiots have loaded up a hair-trigger double-barrelled shit machine gun and the barrel's pointed at your own heads."
—Mr. Lahey's reaction to the rap concert

"That's not my lunch pepperoni you're eating there, is it?"
—Ray sees Ricky eating pepperoni

"He should rap about what he knows, like living in his mom's trailer and eating peanut butter sandwiches."
—Cory trash-talking J-Roc

BAD BOYS SCALE

Free Jiffy Wine attracts fans to J-Roc's rap concert.

Rapper DVS chills after smokin' a fatty.

DVS fires into the air at the rap concert. J-Roc brandishes a piece in his video.

Abducted Rush guitarist Alex Lifeson sits bound awaiting Ricky's song requests, which include "I Like to Rock" and "Diane Sawyer."

nomesayin

The number on the door of the hotel room where Ricky borrowed Alex Lifeson is 2112.

Alex Lifeson's real surname is Zivojinovich. This was the answer for the radio contest to be Alex's guitar tech. Zivojinovich means "son of life."

To avoid detection, Ricky tells Alex that Julian's real name is Gord Downie, who is the lead singer for the Tragically Hip.

The concert scenes were filmed during an actual Rush concert at the Air Canada Centre in Toronto.

Title: CLOSER TO THE HEART
Air Date: MAY 18, 2003

Writers: Mike Clattenburg, John Paul Tremblay, Robb Wells, Jackie Torrens
Director: Mike Clattenburg
Guest Stars: Alex Lifeson (Himself)

It's a big day for Bubbles when his favourite rock group, Rush, comes to town. Bubbles entrusts Ricky with buying him a ticket while he is busy having garbage juice pumped from a kitty's tummy. Meanwhile, Barb cancels Mr. Lahey and Randy's upcoming camping trip until they sort out a ton of recycling that got mixed up with the regular garbage—thanks to you-know-who. Vindictive as ever, Lahey hatches a plan to buy up all the remaining Rush tickets before Bubbles can get any.

Lahey and Randy also steal Bubbles's winning answer to the radio contest to be Rush guitarist Alex Lifeson's guitar technician for the show. They call it in first and Bubbles is screwed again. "Cocksucker!"

"Play that Diane Sawyer song."

Pretending to be Alex's guitar tech, Ricky breaks into his hotel room, wraps him in duct tape and drives him back to the park. If Bubbles can't go to the concert, Ricky will bring the concert to Bubbles. Julian intervenes, and calls a cab to take Alex back to his hotel in exchange for not having Ricky charged.

Cory and Trevor resuscitate Bubbles's excitement when they reveal a secret entrance into the concert venue through the sewer system. Julian sends the two down the manhole—in waterproof suits made from garbage bags—with a bag of dope and a change of clothes taped to their backs. Ricky, Bubbles and Julian follow, only to be removed by backstage security. It's back to the sewers to try again, except this time a brawl breaks out between Ricky, Julian, Randy, Mr. Lahey and concert cops. Alex gets involved and ends up in a trash bin. Bubbles calls a halt to the chaos by playing a giant riff on Alex's guitar. He pledges allegiance as a true Rush fan and security escorts the pretenders, Randy and Mr. Lahey, from the building. Julian pleads with Alex to let Bubbles, the true contest winner, be his guitar tech, even as Ricky squeezes Alex for the joints he thinks are missing from the boys' recovered bag of dope.

The show goes on and so does Bubbles, whose image appears larger than life on the jumbo screen above the concert stage. Afterwards, Alex gives the boys a lift home in his limo. Ricky offers a lame apology for the day's harassment and Bubbles asks Alex to show him some chords. The episode concludes magically, with Alex and Bubbles playing an acoustic duet of "Closer to the Heart."

rare photo
Bubbles beneath the stage at the Rush concert.

"This man's drunk as fuck. He's on drugs. He's a male prostitute."

Alex Lifeson proves to be no match for Ricky's duct-tape and bullshit skills. Driving a car with missing doors was a key factor in the speed and success of the kidnapping. According to Ricky, however, he was just borrowing Mr. Lifeson, and no crime was ever committed.

TRAILER PARK TIPS

Condiment Self-defence

This episode illustrates the devastation an enraged, stupid man can inflict with a squeeze bottle of mustard. Now, not all condiments are equally dangerous. Mustard by far is the deadliest, because it can sting the eyes and leave really bad stains on clothes and skin. Ketchup comes next for its staining ability, but only causes mild eye stinging. On the meeker side we find mayonnaise—and quite frankly, anyone who launches a mayo attack is in way over their head. Relish is the least effective weapon: it stains and sticks poorly and suffers from a limited range of trajectory. For greater condiment safety, please keep your mustard and ketchup bottles barely filled. And if attacked, always turn your head away. As backup, try to keep a mustard-covered hot dog within reach at all times.

All hell breaks loose when Randy refuses to wear a T-shirt offered by Alex Lifeson. Bubbles tries to forcibly dress Randy and the skirmish begins.

BUBBLES

Alex normally performs "Closer to the Heart" with a 12-string guitar; look closely, this duet version is played with two 6-strings.

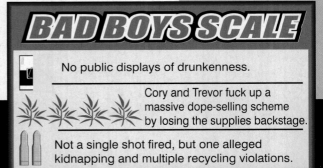

BAD BOYS SCALE

No public displays of drunkenness.

Cory and Trevor fuck up a massive dope-selling scheme by losing the supplies backstage.

Not a single shot fired, but one alleged kidnapping and multiple recycling violations.

Newsflash! Julian rescues Randy from demolished trailer. The park is abuzz.

nomesayin

This episode begins with Ricky addressing the camera, describing his volunteer work at Trinity's school. The first thing that comes to mind, as we listen to Ricky reflect, is that Trinity's school must be pretty hard up for parent volunteers; the second, and more relevant, point is that you can learn a great deal about how the world of economics and business operates just by listening to Ricky's monologues: "I've been helping out at Trinity's school with this this Junior Achievers thing, which is really awesome for the kids 'cause it helps them get their thinking clear about business and shit. It's fuckin' great and I'm learnin' a lot too. It's amazing how much of it applicates to what me and Julian do. Profit counting, supply and command, and all that shit, it's the same whether you are breaking the law or not."

Title: WHERE THE FUCK IS RANDY'S BBQ?
Air Date: MAY 25, 2003

Writers: Mike Clattenburg, John Paul Tremblay, Robb Wells, Jackie Torrens
Director: Mike Clattenburg
Guest Stars: P.J. Crosby (Erica's Daughter), Joseph Rutten (Elderly Man), Shauna MacDonald (Officer Erica Miller)

When Randy and Mr. Lahey confront Ricky as he's BBQing, the assistant trailer park supervisor strongly suggests that Ricky's BBQ is stolen (by Ricky of course) and it belongs to Randy. A denial, a flurry of fuck-offs and a brief scrap ensue—during which Ricky succeeds in putting a shirt on Randy.

A group of kids arrives; it seems Ricky has been helping out at Trinity's school. When he explains his business of reselling BBQs, the kids immediately realize that he in fact steals BBQs and they ask if they can steal some too. Ricky tries to say no, but he's never been one to resist a golden opportunity. Like any responsible adult, Ricky tells the kids that they could go to jail for such activities. The kids, like the quick-thinking, irresponsible kids they are, remind him of the Criminal Youth Justice Act: kids under twelve can't go to jail. "No way. Really?" Ricky replies enviously. Bubbles is a chop-shop artisan with his welding torch, hammer and grinder, reassembling the component parts of the hot BBQs as they come in. But he's horrified when he learns that Ricky is using kids to help him steal BBQs. "Laws are there to protect kids, Ricky!" Yet Ricky and his Junior Achievers continue the hard work of liberating grills from the balconies of nearby apartments—until Ricky is sprayed with mace and has to beat a hasty retreat (with a BBQ in hand).

"We're in the eye of a shiticane, Julian. Ricky is a low-shit system."

While the kids are busy helping Ricky flush his eyes out back at the school, one kid's mom, who happens to be the lovely Constable Erica Miller, shows up. She's the first cop in the show with an IQ higher than your typical golden retriever's. Ricky gives her a bullshit explanation about junior achievement and tells her his name is Randy Lahey. Erica is suspicious and heads to the park, where she meets Lahey and Randy. Julian panics and the boys pitch all the stolen BBQs into the lake, but they float to the surface thanks to the water wings Bubbles attached to them so they wouldn't disappear for good. Fortunately, Julian charms Erica with a show of compassion when he returns Randy's beloved BBQ. Just as it seems things have come to a quiet conclusion, however, Trevor backs the Shitmobile into Lahey's trailer. Lahey runs out wearing an "Indianapolis Jones" costume, but Randy is nowhere to be seen. Julian races heroically into the trailer and pulls Randy—dressed as a giant bumblebee—from under a pile of debris and carries him to safety.

Lahey tries to explain they had been rehearsing for local theatre, but Randy has had enough and he announces that they are gay as fuck! Clearly relieved at being outed at last, Lahey agrees not to press charges. But the real buzz at Sunnyvale begins when a certain police officer enters our hero's trailer for some further interrogation.

rare photo

Mr. Lahey, Randy and their trailer, before Ricky's car smashed it in.

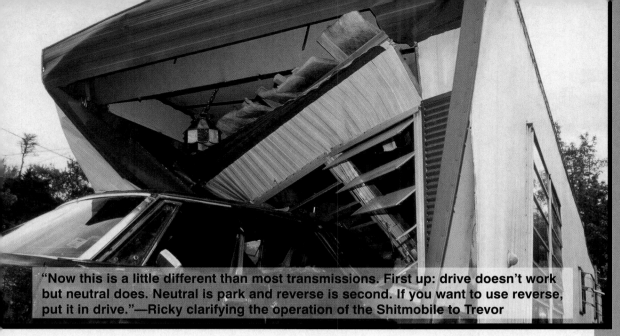

"Now this is a little different than most transmissions. First up: drive doesn't work but neutral does. Neutral is park and reverse is second. If you want to use reverse, put it in drive."—Ricky clarifying the operation of the Shitmobile to Trevor

BEST LINES

"Check this baby out. That there is called a Super Doublebunk-B-Q. I built that myself. I'd like to see that Red, Blue, Green cocksucker put one of those together, duct-taping it."
—Bubbles explaining his BBQ design

"I re-market barbecues."
—Ricky responding to a child's question about what he does for a living

"Many are called, Ricky."
—Lahey, after addressing a cop

"And many can fuck off."
—Ricky in reply

RICKYISMS

"Lahey was my mother's mating name."
—Ricky explaining to Constable Miller why there are so many Laheys in the park

"Why the fuck are you dressed up like Indianapolis Jones?"
—Ricky queries Mr. Lahey on his "theatre" outfit

Officer Erica Miller is fresh on the Sunnyvale scene with a no-nonsense approach to police work. Well, maybe a little nonsense, when she corners Julian for questioning.

BAD BOYS SCALE

Mr. Lahey appears to be very drunk the entire episode. Okay, he is very drunk.

Julian explains Ricky's problems to Erica by blaming the dope.

No gunfire but plenty of illegal grill grabbin' and very close brushes with the law.

Julian strikes a Georges Vézina pose. Looks like the gloves may have actually belonged to the hockey great too.

nomesayin

When Bubbles busts the boys out of jail, he tells them to be quiet as he removes the orange road-hockey ball (gag) from Julian's mouth, but leaves the one in Ricky's. Good thinking, Bubs! Julian doesn't even spill his drink as he collapses unconscious to the ground after being shot by Lahey's stun gun.

MR. LAHEY'S SHIT ANALOGIES

"Randy, the shit pool is getting full and we better strain it before it overflows and causes a shit slide that covers the whole community. I will not have a Pompeian catastrophe happening to our community."

"We're going to nail those shidiots."

Title: THE DELUSIONS OF OFFICER JIM LAHEY
Air Date: JUNE 1, 2003

Writers: Mike Clattenburg, John Paul Tremblay, Robb Wells, Jackie Torrens
Director: Mike Clattenburg
Guest Stars: George Green (Officer George Green), Shauna MacDonald (Officer Erica Miller), Francine Deschepper (Travel Agent)

The boys are enjoying a spirited game of road hockey, and this one's happening right in front of Lahey's trailer. Things are getting nasty between the Shirts and the Skins, with Ricky directing a steady stream of verbal abuse at Trevor's team. Lahey watches from behind the plastic drop sheet erected where the front of his trailer used to be. Today's the anniversary of the day he was kicked off the force and he's feeling mighty low.

"I'm getting drunk today. Big time."

Randy is trying to help by making Mr. Lahey "comfort food" and putting buttercups in his ice cube trays (a trick he learned from the Designer Guys). But an errant hockey ball (fired by Ricky, of course) rips through the plastic and smashes into Lahey's old uniform case. Broken glass sprays about the room and peppers his buttercup-cubed drink with razor-sharp shards. This is the last straw. He snaps. "I'm getting drunk today," is all he can manage to say. "Big time." Lahey, once completely wasted, dons his old uniform, toupée and gun. He and his reluctant deputy, Randy, take to the streets. At the liquor store, while Randy is loading up on coolers inside, Lahey drops a cigarette into his lap and spills his drink. He flings open the New Yorker's giant door just as a thief runs past and KOs the would-be robber. The manager calls Lahey a hero and you can almost (but not quite) see a dim flicker of twisted purpose light up in Jim's alcohol-soaked mind.

When he and Randy get back to Sunnyvale, they mount a motorcycle and sidecar straight out of Hogan's Heroes and circle the park announcing that the federal government has declared Sunnyvale a town and they are its official police force. Lahey converts a shed into a jail, smashes the shit out of J-Roc's ghetto blaster and sets out in search of Ricky with the maniacal determination of Jack Torrance at the end of The Shining. Ricky and Julian soon find themselves behind bars, bound at the wrist and muffled with orange gag balls courtesy of Officer Jim Lahey.

With Randy's help, Bubbles frees them both and calls the cops. In fact, Randy is so troubled that he subdues his beloved—and shotgun-wielding—Mr. Lahey with a stun gun. As sirens approach in the distance, Randy convinces Julian not to press charges. Peace, however stable, reigns in Sunnyvale.

rare photo

Mr. Lahey at his most delusional. Randy at his regular hungry.

Ricky, Julian and Bubbles. Sunnyvale Trailer Park Road Hockey League's most feared line.

"Kojak's got a wig on."
—J-Roc observing Lahey in his police uniform and toupée

"Even if Lahey is a cop, he's got nothing on us."
—Bubbles

"Well Randy, so far we have five counts of gas siphoning, forty-two counts of weapons discharging, sixty-seven counts of lewd and obnoxious behaviour, and one hundred counts of theft under a thousand dollars."
—Lahey

RICKYISM

"I've been fucked over from being electramacuted."
—Ricky, after being zapped by Lahey's stun gun.

◄ Julian and Bubbles demonstrate that the Sunnyvale Trailer Park Road Hockey League protective headgear rule is optional.

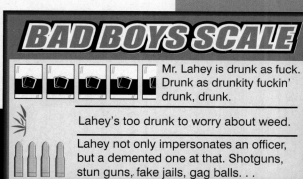

BAD BOYS SCALE

Mr. Lahey is drunk as fuck. Drunk as drunkity fuckin' drunk, drunk.

Lahey's too drunk to worry about weed.

Lahey not only impersonates an officer, but a demented one at that. Shotguns, stun guns, fake jails, gag balls. . .

Trevor prefers a sheer hose while Cory likes the support of control top.

nomesayin

MR. LAHEY'S SHIT ANALOGIES

"When a shit apple falls from a tree, it has no choice, just like Trinity."

"Captain Shitacular is raising shit in Sunnyvale again."

"Look what we've got, Randy—shit stormtroopers."

"Looks like you've fucked your shit goose this time."

Title: A SHIT LEOPARD CAN'T CHANGE HIS SPOTS
Air Date: JUNE 8, 2003

Writers: Mike Clattenburg, John Paul Tremblay, Robb Wells, Jackie Torrens, Barrie Dunn
Director: Mike Clattenburg
Guest Stars: George Green (Officer George Green), Shauna MacDonald (Officer Erica Miller), Jacob Rolfe (Jacob)

Ricky finally realizes he needs to start making up for all the years of being a shitty, negligent father. To this end, he's been spending quality time with Trinity, patiently explaining why throwing garbage in the lake is not littering and showing her how to steal tires. He even organizes a Christmas dinner with gifts—at a picnic bench . . . in the middle of summer.

"I'm drunk as fuck."

Julian announces that it's almost time to go on the cruise they've been working towards all year; they just need to pick up the eight tickets from the travel agency. Ricky is actually conflicted: he's always in jail over winter and normally will miss spending holiday time with the family, so he's holding the holidays well in advance. The timing of the cruise couldn't be worse. Yet, when the boys arrive, the agent only has seven tickets for them. Turns out, Ricky neglected to return the travel agent's phone calls in order to collect the special offer for the eighth (buy seven, get one free) promotional ticket. And Julian neglected to tell Ricky that Erica was coming on the cruise. The boys need another $4,200. Unless they leave Cory and Trevor behind…

Not surprisingly, Lahey is doing his best to fuck it all up for Ricky and brings in the police (during Christmas dinner) to evict him, citing multiple lease violations. Furious at this happening in front of Trinity, Ricky freaks out and throws the turkey at Lahey's car.

Life at Sunnyvale has become too much of a hassle for Ricky and he decides jail is better than the park: "At least jail is nice and warm in the winter." So he heads into town to get himself arrested. He declares his drunkeness to the world, fires his gun to attract cops and throws bottles at the police station, but no one notices. Even Erica, who can't stand Ricky, refuses to arrest him. Finally he goes to a variety store, announces right into the ATM's camera that he is stealing the machine and drags it down the street with a pick-up truck.

When Julian, Lahey and Randy open the ATM and get covered in dye, Erica must choose between love and duty. She busts them all and they go to jail. Ricky becomes the new park supervisor and gets to look forward to real Christmas with Trinity. Cory, Trevor, Sarah, Lucy and Bubs hit the high seas!

rare photo
Bubbles and Julian can't stop Ricky. He's missing jail, but no matter how hard he tries, he can't get arrested.

Bubbles hits the high seas–or is it the seas high?

RICKYISMS

"The fastest way to get money is to steal a bank machine. It doesn't take rocket appliances to realize all you gotta do is take a fuckin' chain, hook it up to a truck and yank the fuckin' bank machine out of the store."
—Ricky's version of personal banking

"What I started realizing about Trinity is now she's at this age that it's gorilla see, gorilla do, and what I'm doing, she starts to do. If I throw a bottle in the lake, she's going to throw a bottle in the lake, which is no big deal."
—Damn dirty apes

◄ Ricky usually misses Christmas dinner with his family each year because he's in jail. Not this year. He's having Christmas dinner in the summer.

BAD BOYS SCALE

Ricky is fairly drunk the entire episode.

Ricky says he is drunk and full of dope. No obvious consumption.

Lots of theft, robberies, two gunshots fired and a laundromat taken to the cleaners for all of their loose change by gun-wielding Cory and Trevor.

105

TRAILER PARK BOYS
Postcards from the Park

A Sunnyvale-Compton drive by lasts about 23 seconds.

Sarah and Lucy keepin' it real.
Except for the boobs, of course.

Ricky can't break free from Phil's gravitational mass.

Jail and
Bubbles
don't mix.

Move over Thelma and Louise.

SEASON 4

Title: NEVER CRY SHITWOLF
Air Date: APRIL 11, 2004

Writers: Mike Clattenburg, John Paul Tremblay, Robb Wells, Mike Smith
Director: Mike Clattenburg
Guest Stars: George Green (Officer George Green)

Julian, Randy and Mr. Lahey are riding the bus back to Sunnyval out of jail at last. Unfortunately for Trailer Park Supervisor Rick they're out early. Ricky calls his hash hockey game with Bubbles to halt and sets to work clearing any traces of the illegal activities th have occupied his months as supervisor. To buy some time, he senc Assistant Trailer Park Supervisor Bubbles, who is drunk and stone to distract Julian and keep him away from his trailer until Ricky (we Cory and Trevor, with a crudely written list of tasks) can clear out th massive dope-growing operation. Ricky is clearly panicked, and high gear thanks to the three cigarettes he's smoking simultaneous

"Fuck, I missed jail this year."

Julian soon approaches the large plywood gate Ricky has erected the park entrance to keep out unwanted visitors, like cops. Julian ju wants to go home, but Bubbles and Ricky convince him to join the for drinks first. As Julian's homesickness grows, Bubbles's attemp to divert him become increasingly desperate. He talks Julian in taking a ride in his "new car" to go get some chicken. Bubbles ha actually swapped J-Roc some hash to borrow his pimp new rid But even the car's cool rum-and-cola dispenser—the converte windshield washer—isn't enough to keep Julian interested. S Bubbles pleads with him to come by the shed so he can sing him new song. Poor drunken Bubbles's lies are wearing thin, and h strums an old standard about kitties that Julian has heard before.

Meanwhile Randy and Mr. Lahey learn that they are no long employed by Sunnyvale and Ricky sends them to live in their ca Vowing revenge, Mr. Lahey suspects Ricky is growing dope aga and calls in the cops to bust him. Ricky tries to stall the cops outsic the Sunnyvale gate, with everyone else in tow. Bubbles, the drunke troubadour, becomes belligerent with the cops and anyone else wh will listen to his suddenly abusive songs. Ricky negotiates a limite trailer search by Officer George Green and his crew. They find r dope, of course, and Mr. Lahey endures George's "Never cry shitwo lecture. Bubbles, however, spends a night in the drunk tank aft playing one chord too many. Julian accompanies him, like the goc friend he is, but also takes the opportunity to grill Bubbles abo whether Ricky's growing dope. Bubbles is reluctant to rat Ricky ou so Julian convinces him to blink "twice for yes."

Ricky's term as trailer park supervisor was successful; he avoided assassination, at least.

nomesayin

Ricky's to-do list for dope relocation:

1. Steal a 5-ton truck
2. Get boxes and tape
3. Move dope equipment into boxes
4. Put boxes into truck
5. Take the truck away
6. Tell Cory and Trevor to fuck off

J-Roc and posse's chicken order:

J-Roc: Chicken-and-rib combo with extra roll
T: Quarter-chicken dinner with extra gravy
DVS: Small chicken dinner with french fries and onion rings

rare photo

Randy, Mr. Lahey and their new living quarters: the New Yorker.

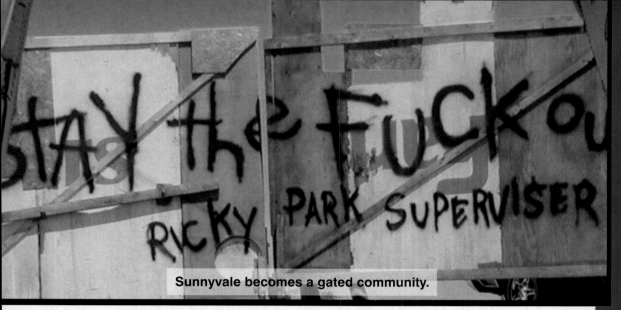

Sunnyvale becomes a gated community.

RICKYISMS

"Do onto others as you do onto you."
—One of the ten commandments Ricky brought down from Mount Fuck Up

"Do you have a search warranty?"
—Good to have in case the cops break something

Bubbles's drunken performance of his kitty song fails to distract Julian.

BUBBLES'S KITTY SONG
Kitties are so nice, get them down,
spin them 'round, tickle their bellies . . .

Bubbles is so drunk he's arrested. Plus, an in-car rum and cola dispenser.

Lots of great hash hockey. Ricky hides the dope operation from Julian and the cops.

No gunfire, but one drug search and a public intoxication arrest.

109

Title: A MAN'S GOTTA EAT
Air Date: APRIL 18, 2004

Writers: Mike Clattenburg, John Paul Tremblay, Robb Wells, Mike Smith, Iain MacLeod
Director: Mike Clattenburg
Guest Stars: Shauna MacDonald (Officer Erica Miller), Paul MacLeod (Man in Suit), Glen Grant (Satellite Employee)

Ricky's dubious tenure as trailer park supervisor becomes a little more dubious when a technician arrives to disconnect all the illegal satellite TV hookups Ricky's been selling to the residents. "I'm paying ten fucking dollars a month!" Sunnyvale's disembodied voice Donny reminds him. Ricky argues that the feed comes free from space and that the TV company should be paying him for allowing the signal into the park. Space, after all, is owned by "Naysa."

Julian, with no money—Ricky has run up his credit cards—and an empty foil-lined trailer, decides to leave. Ricky offers him the supervisor's car (with a barrel of swish in the trunk) to live in, which Julian accepts, but then he leaves anyway. Meanwhile, Randy faces his own deprivations in love, finance, housing and cheeseburgers. He dons his old working clothes and persona—Smokey the male prostitute—and hits the road. Mr. Lahey decides that if he can't afford a burger to lure his man back, he'll hunt one down, and fashions a crude bow and arrow.

Smokey workin' it on the streets.

nomesayin

"Swish. My fuck, does it ever get you some drunk."

At the donair shop, Randy—er, Smokey—agrees to a $10 job. But it's a sting! And Julian's ex Erica Miller is the cop. Before she can bust Smokey, they stumble across Julian, uncharacteristically hammered and hugging and kissing a stray dog while eating pizza crusts from a dumpster. Bubbles wheels in, with a football-helmeted Ricky in tow, and Erica finds the whole scene so pathetic she can't bring herself to arrest anybody. Bubbles tries to sober up Julian with a better rum.

Cleaned up and sporting Bubbles's eighties vintage parachute pants, Julian makes peace with his buddies. Ricky even hires Randy to get Julian's trailer in order—the pay, two cheeseburgers. But when Randy discovers Ricky eating his earnings, the boys go at it. Mr. Lahey happens upon their grappling from a misleading angle and fires an arrow into Ricky's shoulder. Moments later, they've cleared up the misunderstanding and Randy accepts Mr. Lahey's offering of a blue-jay cheeseburger.

Ricky and Bubbles decide it's time to come clean with Julian and sheepishly take him to their "super dope" field. Ricky developed the fast-growing strain when he got bored of his supervisor duties. Julian's apprehension quickly turns into grand plans. "Maybe we'll buy an island with a Ferris wheel," says Ricky. "No, something better," replies Julian. "We're gonna buy the trailer park."

Ricky's list of occupations in which people need to be stoned to perform:

1. Carpenters
2. Electricians
3. Dishwashers
4. Floor cleaners
5. Lawyers
6. Doctors
7. Politicians
8. CBC employees
9. Principals
10. People who paint lines on the road

rare photo

Mr. Lahey hunting for Randy's burger meat. Ends up bagging a blue jay.

Better days are ahead for Julian.

Blue Jay Bisque

Mr. Lahey and Randy will be the first to tell you that a blue jay makes a great burger, but for those who want to experience the full culinary pleasure of the bird, we suggest the following tasty, and certainly tempting, recipe.

A hearty soup for those cool autumn evenings. You'll need:

- 6 large blue jays
- 1 onion
- 3 carrots
- 2 celery stalks
- fresh thyme
- 2 cups of white wine
- 2 cups of water
- 1 cup of cream

1. Remove blue jay feathers, head and organs.
2. Lightly season birds and place in roasting pan.
3. Brown slightly in butter or oil along with vegetables.
4. Add wine and water, then cover and roast in oven at 325 degrees or on hot Shitmobile engine for about two hours, or until the cocksucker's done.
5. Strain liquid through sieve or Trevor's shirt into pan. Don't throw that out—it's the part you'll be eating.
6. Whisk the cream into warm pan. Use brush or comb if you don't have a whisk.
7. Garnish with sprig of thyme on top and blue jay feather on the side.

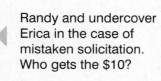

Randy and undercover Erica in the case of mistaken solicitation. Who gets the $10?

BAD BOYS SCALE

Julian is drunk as fuck. Mr. Lahey is drunk as always. Bubbles cleans the swish out of Julian with rum.

Ricky reveals his field of "super dope."

Mr. Lahey shoots Ricky with a homemade arrow. Randy's a male prostitute.

J-Roc makes a critical career move.

nomesayin

Rub 'n Tiz'zug Do's and Don'ts for Cory and Trevor

DON'T converse with clients to make them feel at ease. Keeping quiet and looking away might be the best option.

DO try to look skinnier than you already are and blend in with nearby hockey sticks, or you will be conscripted into service by the boys as "sensual" massage workers. If you must go into battle, no hockey talk while handling weapons.

DON'T complain when the boys hand you this job. Just put on your gloves, get to work and think of England.

DO mention latex allergies. The last thing the boys need is an allergic reaction from one of their workers on the job.

DON'T skimp on the oil. Any job worth doing is also a job worth doing well. 10w30 will work in a pinch.

Title: RUB 'N TIZ'ZUG
Air Date: APRIL 25, 2004

Writers: Mike Clattenburg, John Paul Tremblay, Robb Wells, Mike Smith
Director: Mike Clattenburg
Guest Stars: Jacob Rolfe (Jacob), Bernard Robichaud (Cyrus), Trina Hennick (Government Woman), Tara Doyle (Massage Lady), Shawn Duggan (Government Man), Novalea Buchan (Police Officer), Richard Collins (Motel Manager)

'Twas nighttime at Sunnyvale and in Bubbles's shed, a show about samsquanches filled him with dread. Poor ol' Julian's asleep on his trailer floor, then later awakes and shakes Bubbles's door. Bubbles calls Ricky, his voice filled with fear, and tells him to "Get the fuck over here." Ricky's been watching those Saskatchewans too, picks up a bat, he knows what to do. Julian, draped in bedding that looks like a pelt, yanks at the door—fuck, Bubbles needs help! They spring from their shed and trailer well armed, and beat down that samsquanch, do him some harm. But the beast is tough and resists attack, grabbing the bat and fighting them back. But the boys are determined and knock him down, and to their wondering eyes, fuck, that's Julian on the ground.

The boys wake up bruised and swollen from last night's mix-up. Bandaged in duct tape, they head out in the Shitmobile to steal office furniture for Julian's empty trailer. Posing as movers, the boys walk into an office and start hauling out furniture, promising replacements are on the way. "Just ask Jeff or Mike," says Ricky hoping to hit on a name. Their successful getaway inspires Julian. The boys proceed to a local motel—staffed by a portly gentleman who's paranoid about people staring at his gut—to divest it of beds and such. The boys are opening a massage parlour.

"I don't play jail."

Back at the park, J-Roc and his new manager, DVS, connect the boys with some lovely staff for the parlour. Lines form as soon as the business opens, and Julian calls for reinforcements. Short-staffed in the meantime, he hands Cory and Trevor latex gloves and orders them to work. Sarah shows up just as they are kicked out by a customer (angry-voiced Donny) and complains to Julian about the working conditions. Soon, Cyrus arrives at the park with his typical ballistic entrance—it turns out he manages the new ladies. He also confronts the boys for spray-painting his Corvette, but they're too sore to fight. Fortunately Randy is nearby and it's off with the pants. Randy hammers Cyrus but good.

When the cops show up, DVS convinces J-Roc that this is his moment to establish street cred for his upcoming CD release. J-Roc flashes a piece and takes the heat for the entire operation. Camera at the ready, DVS makes sure the moment is framed just right.

rare photo

Sunnyvale's only massage parlour gets busted, putting these ladies and Cory and Trevor out of work.

The morning after the boys beat each other with baseball bats . . . by mistake.

"No more shit talk 'til we're back in power."
—Lahey doesn't like Randy talkin' shit

"Kiss my hand. Say 'I'm a little bitch'."
—Randy pummels Cyrus and gets him to say uncle, more or less

"Why don't we fuck ON?"
—Cyrus

RICKYISM

"Get two birds stoned at once."
—Ricky doesn't want to kill the birds, just fuck them up a bit

Mr. Lahey survives an early-morning attack of leftover chicken fingers.

BAD BOYS SCALE

 No one's too thirsty.

Low-smoke episode.

 J-Roc stages his own arrest with gratuitous handgun waving. Cyrus fires a gun to announce his arrival. Lots of stolen furniture and an illegal brothel.

Title: THE GREEN BASTARD
Air Date: MAY 2, 2004

Writers: Mike Clattenburg, John Paul Tremblay, Robb Wells, Mike Smith
Director: Mike Clattenburg
Guest Stars: Jacob Rolfe (Jacob), Jerry Strum (Taxi Driver), Miles Meili (Bernie Sanford), Jeffrey Jones (Jason Maloney)

Celebration is already on tap for Sunnyvale's Community Day when Mr. Lahey learns he's going to win the Trailer Park Supervisor of the Year Award. There's only one problem: Ricky has his job. Lahey spiffs himself up and pleads with Barb to pretend that he's supervisor when the delegates arrive, explaining that the award will be good for Sunnyvale and may help them join the Trailer Park Union, adding value to the park. Speaking of value, Ricky has set up some pretty enticing amusements for Community Day—an event he's planned to generate cash for the boys' deposit on the park. There are front-end loader rides and a paintball range—where kids are strafing Cory and Trevor unmercifully, for $2 a shot. Bubbles is ecstatic to learn about the day's biggest attraction: a "wrestling" ring. He races back to the shed to transform himself into the Green Bastard, from "parts unknown."

"Green Bastard . . . parts unknown!"

Meanwhile, Bernie Sanford, the president of the International Association of Trailer Parks, Trailer Park Supervisors and Assistant Trailer Park Supervisors (IAOTPTPSAATPS) and his entourage arrive. Barb has agreed to Jim's charade, but Ricky hasn't. Almost on cue, Ricky shows up and, as supervisor, insists the "dickheads' in the suits need to move their vehicles. When they don't, Ricky pisses on one of their cars. Bernie confronts him and threatens to bring out "the right hook." Eventually, all parties agree to a tag-team wrestling challenge: Randy and Mr. Lahey versus Ricky and the Green Bastard. Winners run the park.

When Randy, curiously glowing a Hulk-like green, enters the ring, Ricky gets the best of him but accidentally clobbers Sanford, who is acting as referee. Mr. Lahey takes advantage and slips a foreign object to Randy, who takes Ricky down. Bubbles sees the treachery and jumps into the ring just as the association president comes around. Sanford disqualifies the boys, and Lahey and Randy take charge once again.

Ricky is furious, and Bubbles calls Mr. Lahey and Randy "cheated cheatingtons." So when Lahey receives a new (used) Cadillac with his award, Ricky trashes Sanford and posse's cars with the front-end loader. The association president storms off—Sunnyvale is just not ready to be part of the union. Julian calms Ricky down and assures him it's all for the best, because now they can spend more time on their dope field. Bubbles "wrastles" until dark, eventually wearing out all comers.

Looks like trouble for the Green Bastard when Trevor the Elongated Skeleton applies a rear naked choke during Sunnyvale's Community Day celebration.

nomesayin

The price of fun at Sunnyvale's Community Day:

$35:
The cost for "Anyone Fight" with the trailer park supervisor and the assistant trailer park supervisor in the makeshift "wrastling" ring.

$30:
"Frunt End Loader Rides."

$12:
Chicken and liquor.

$2:
Cost per shot at the paintball firing range, which features Trevor and Cory wearing garbage-bag bull's eyes.

rare photo

Cory and Trevor present a real challenge as moving targets for the kids' paintball firing range.

Barb can't believe she's in the same room as The Incredible Bulk.

RICKYISM

"Look, I know right now I'm supposed to swallow my prize, but I'm fuckin' pissed off, man. They cheated and that's bullshit."
—Ricky doesn't like losing to Randy and Mr. Lahey in the ring

The much-anticipated women's match between Lucy and Sarah was never televised.

BAD BOYS SCALE

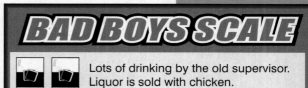

Lots of drinking by the old supervisor. Liquor is sold with chicken.

 Little to report from weed central.

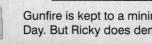 Gunfire is kept to a minimum on Community Day. But Ricky does demolish several cars.

Title: CONKY
Air Date: MAY 9, 2004

Writers: Mike Clattenburg, John Paul Tremblay, Robb Wells, Mike Smith
Director: Mike Clattenburg
Guest Stars: George Green (Officer George Green), Nicola Lipman (Nurse), Sam Tarasco (Sam Losco), Ian Tench (Orderly)

The show begins with Bubbles suffering from an abscessed tooth and trying to cope with an unruly herd of cats: "There are just too many of you around. Your parents are banging like crazy." Desperate, he ties his tooth to the shed door and throws it open. Too bad Ricky's nose blocks the door. Before he regains his bearings, Ricky adheres a freshly glued model truck to one hand and a glue-soaked rag to his bloodied nose.

Bubs hates hospitals and refuses to go for help about his tooth. He hasn't been to one since he had Conky to comfort him. In grade six, Julian explains, Bubbles made a large hand puppet named Conky. Ricky, seething, adds that Bubbles's puppet "fucked up his mind." Mr. Lahey arrives and tells Bubbles to get his "shit rats" under control or he'll be evicted from the park, which distresses Bubbles further. Julian concludes the only way to get his friend to a hospital is to find Conky. In a steaming swamp, a cursing Ricky recovers the "corpse" of the malicious puppet, and reunites "little fuck face" with his overjoyed creator. Conky immediately begins to hurl verbal abuse at Ricky, who warns him, "Fuck with me and I'll fuck with you."

Disturbed from peaceful his slumber, Conky isn't happy.

nomesayin

MR. LAHEY'S SHIT ANALOGIES

"Those two shit rats just pissed on forty dollars worth of eclairs at the bake sale and Stinkster and Daisy were doing it in front of the kids."
—Lahey complaining to Bubbles about his cats

"Goddamn shit monkeys."—Lahey altering the species slightly

"Ricky, you are pointing a loaded handgun at a puppet."

They get to the hospital, but Ricky and Conky's feud soon gets them all expelled from the emergency room (after Ricky tells the entire hospital to fuck off). Bubbles, in constant pain, seems unable to control the malevolent puppet. The boys drop by Sam Losco's newly reopened veterinary practice and find Mr. Lahey and Randy negotiating a price for "dealing with" the cat problem. In a rage, Bubbles attacks Mr. Lahey. Ricky, still hallucinating from the glue, starts shooting, and Sam returns fire with tranquilizer darts, striking Ricky, Randy and Mr. Lahey. Ricky, exhibiting his infamous tolerance for drugs, remains conscious and the boys demand Losco extract the tooth. A spontaneous staring contest brings Ricky and Conky's bad blood to a head. Ricky points his gun directly between the bespectacled eyes of his nemesis. Julian reminds him that Conky is just Bubbles, but then Conky calls Julian "Patrick Swayze" and starts singing the theme to the movie *Ghost*. Julian blows the evil little fucker's head right off.

Using quick thinking, dog-urine samples and Julian's drink before the cops arrive, the boys manage to lay all the blame for the gunfire directly on the sopping crotches of the unconscious Mr. Lahey and Randy. The show ends with Bubbles proudly displaying his successfully removed tooth, and the return of Conky to his steaming grave.

rare photo

Sam Losco restores order in his veterinary clinic.

Ricky looks like he's been in a fight with a matador. The end is near for Conky.

BEST LINES

"Well, now I can't smoke, that's my first problem. I have a busted nose, which I have a rag glued to, and a fuckin' truck stuck to my hand. How's that for a start?"
—Ricky at the nurses' desk

"And he's fucked in the head. He needs a brain transplant."
—Conky completing Ricky's diagnosis

"Julian, I can't be responsible for every little thing that comes out of his mouth, you know."
—Bubbles

"You are not going to listen to Ricky, are you Bubbles? You're a lot smarter than he is. You just remember, I call the shots around here."
—Conky

"I thought you were dead, too, you little bastard!"
—Ricky

"Luckily, I don't need oxygen to live underwater like you do . . . Stupid."
—Conky

Bubbles and the B-17

"One time, I was making a model and I glued the wing of a B-17 bomber to my bird by accident. Remember that time I was walking funny for a couple of weeks? I had a wing on my bird."
—Bubbles explaining the perils of using contact cement

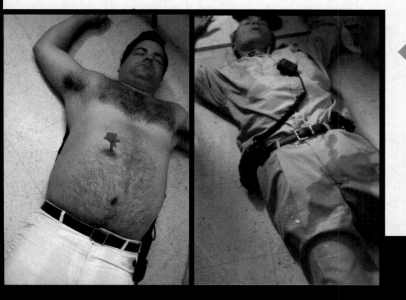

"Randy, it looks like you pissed yourself, boy."
"Looks like you pissed yourself too, Mr. Lahey."

BAD BOYS SCALE

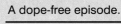

Julian's drink, tranquilizer darts and dog urine, not alcohol, land Randy and Mr. Lahey in the drunk tank.

A dope-free episode.

Killing Conky by handgun should be a 5 out of 5. But Sam using tranquilizer darts instead of bullets makes it a 4.

SEASON 4 EPISODE 6

Title: IF YOU LOVE SOMETHING, SET IT FREE
Air Date: MAY 16, 2004

Writers: Mike Clattenburg, John Paul Tremblay, Robb Wells, Mike Smith
Director: Mike Clattenburg

Someone or something has been messing with the boys' dope field. Determined to seize the culprit, they arm Cory and Trevor with homemade potato guns and send them into the towering plants. Ricky, of course, gets shot in the process. Moments later, they emerge clawed, beaten and terrified. It's a samsquanch, Bubbles insists. Ever compassionate, he dresses Trevor's chest wounds with a potato chip bag—unfortunately they were salt and vinegar chips. Back home, Sarah is not pleased with Cory and Trevor's condition as they emerge from the trunk of Ricky's car. Ricky demands smokes from Trevor and Sarah demands the same. The tension is palpable, but Sarah wins and Cory and Trevor follow her home.

"You look kinda French with your little moustache, there. I'm gonna call you Steve French."

It's back to the field with a net. Bubbles slips in poop. They're close. When they find the weed bandit, he's no samsquanch, but a mountain lion—or in Bubbles's eyes, a big, misunderstood, baked kitty: "We're taking him back to the trailer park and putting him through rehab." Bubbles puts a leash on the big cat and names him Steve French.

They decide to hide Steve under J-Roc's mom's trailer until they can figure out what to do with him. There they discover J-Roc hiding out with DVS and Tyrone. Apparently J-Roc was only sentenced to community service for the massage parlour incident, and community service doesn't sell records.

Steve French gets the munchies and finds Randy's uncooked burgers, complete with Viagra seasoning. ("Mr. Lahey, a tiger ate all my burgers.") With a full belly and a chemically inspired libido, Steve happens upon Trevor in a leopard-skin vest. Close enough. He chases Trevor into Mr. Lahey's trailer. Moments later, Trevor runs home an emotional wreck and wearing barely a stitch.

Lucy and Sarah are pissed that Ricky and the boys are allowing a mountain lion to roam the park with kids around and threaten to call the cops. Bubbles knows he has to wean Steve off the dope, so he asks Julian for some fajitas, which he turns into "weedjitas." If Bubbles straightens this big kitty out, maybe he can stay. But Ricky and Julian convince Bubbles that Steve must return to the wild, and he agrees to let him go—but says that if he comes back, he belongs to him forever. Steve knows he has it good, and doesn't leave—until a foxy female mountain lion lures him back to the forest. Bubbles fights back tears, and so do Ricky and Julian, even if they won't admit it.

Trevor's relationship with Steve French gets off to a rough start.

nomesayin

MR. LAHEY'S SHIT ANALOGIES

"The Shit Abyss."

"Tracks lead right to Shit Town."

"There's no fool like an old fool, Leshiticus."

rare photo
Steve French, obviously stoned.

One of the more disturbing moments at Sunnyvale as Trevor, well . . . um . . .

RICKYISMS

"Clear to see who makes the pants here."
—Ricky loses the "Trevor smokes" battle to Sarah

"What if he had radies?"
—Radies: when insects foam at the mouth

"You're trying to fill my feet."
—Makes it tough to walk a mile in Ricky's shoes

"He's just a little kitty who's hooked on the weed."

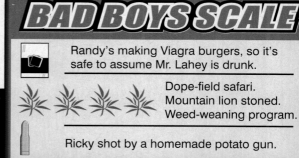

BAD BOYS SCALE

Randy's making Viagra burgers, so it's safe to assume Mr. Lahey is drunk.

Dope-field safari. Mountain lion stoned. Weed-weaning program.

Ricky shot by a homemade potato gun.

Title: PROPANE, PROPANE
Air Date: MAY 23, 2004

Writers: Mike Clattenburg, John Paul Tremblay, Robb Wells, Mike Smith
Director: Mike Clattenburg
Guest Stars: Jon Loverin (Driving Instructor), Stan Carew (Radio Announcer)

Big plans mean big rigs, and Cory and Trevor have stolen one filled with propane. The boys plan to sell the fuel in the park and then fill the truck with weed to be sold at the big "Snoopy Dog" concert in Moncton. All they need now are Ray's licence plates and a big-rig driver's licence for Bubbles. Once Julian and Ricky bribe the driving instructor with hash, the plan is almost foolproof.

To divert Lahey's attention while they drive the rig past his trailer, the boys leave Lone Ranger and Tonto costumes on top of the trash. Meanwhile, Barb has big plans of her own: she's intent on marrying Ricky and asks Jim for her diamond ring back. Jim, looking for a bit of security himself, thinks Barb wants to get back together with him. He cleans up and heads to Barb's trailer to propose. Barb not only turns him down, but strips him of his duties, evicts him from his trailer and mentions she's going to marry his arch enemy. Bad day for Jim.

"Holy fuck, I love licorice."

Bubbles returns from his driving test more excited than Chet Atkins pullin' gears on his custom Kenworth. Sadly, the bribed instructor refuses to give him a licence: "He can't see fuck all." Depressed, Bubbles scolds his eyes for letting him down. But Ricky won't be dissuaded—he puts together a fake licence and lies to Julian about Bubbles's test. Everything is back on track.

Ricky's out to the field next for dope testing, and man is this product potent. He then heads to Barb's, who greets him warmly with a handful of licorice. Her offerings overwhelm Ricky and he agrees to marry her. Julian and Bubbles advise against this, as do a series of dark portents —Ricky falls for a smokes-and-pepperoni-baited trap and then almost gets electrocuted while deep-frying a turkey.

Bad news. The cops have been finding dope fields in the area. The unease intensifies when Mr. Lahey shows up stumbling drunk and pissing himself to buy propane. That evening, as Ricky prepares a bath, Barb steps out to investigate the smell of propane around her trailer. Moments later, a crazed Mr. Lahey runs behind the trailer carrying a bow and burning arrows. He shoots one at Barb's trailer and it explodes. She screams, "Ricky!"

. . . to be continued.

The Lone Lahey.

nomesayin

MR. LAHEY'S SHIT ANALOGIES

"He grew up as a little shitspark, from the ol' shitflame, and then he turned into a shit bonfire, and then, driven by the winds of his monumental ignorance, he turned into a raging shitfire storm. I can unleash a shitnami tidal wave that'll engulf Ricky and extinguish his shitflames forever, and with any luck he'll drown in the undershit of the waves . . . Shitwaves."

rare photo
Bubbles almost gets his big-rig license. But once again, his eyes fuck him over.

Randy running bare.

RICKYISMS

"Peach and cake."
—Ricky's idea of easy bake?

"What Julian doesn't grow won't burn him."
—Ricky not wanting to ignite an argument

"He passed with flying fucking carpets."
—Ricky lies to Julian about Bubbles's driving test

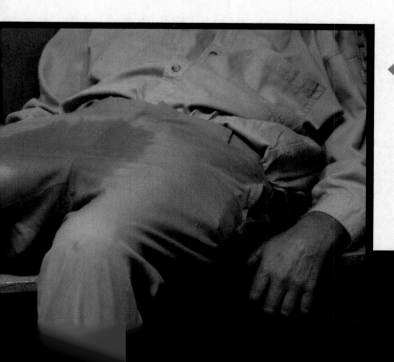

◀ Mr. Lahey consumes so much alcohol, his pee is as flammable as propane.

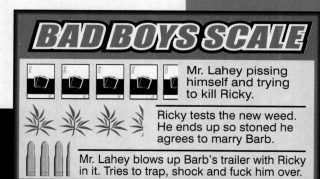

BAD BOYS SCALE

Mr. Lahey pissing himself and trying to kill Ricky.

Ricky tests the new weed. He ends up so stoned he agrees to marry Barb.

Mr. Lahey blows up Barb's trailer with Ricky in it. Tries to trap, shock and fuck him over.

No worries—does this look like a man who can shoot straight?

nomesayin

MR. LAHEY'S SHIT ANALOGIES

"Tick tock, tick tock . . . Shitclock's ticking, Ricky."

Cory and Trevor's Dope Harvest Rules:

1. Cut down the weed.
2. Bundle in neat piles and put in bags.
3. Keep in radio contact.
4. Don't fuck nothing up.

Title: WORKIN' MAN
Air Date: MAY 30, 2004

Writers: Mike Clattenburg, John Paul Tremblay, Robb Wells, Mike Smith
Director: Mike Clattenburg
Guest Stars: Rita MacNeil (Herself), George Green (Officer George Green), Bill Wood (Courier), Nancy Regan (Reporter), Novalea Buchan (Police Officer)

He's missing some hair, but otherwise Ricky has survived Mr. Lahey's attempt to blow him up, thanks to a "fire-retarded" bathtub. Now it's time to beat the cops and harvest that weed. Mr. Lahey, meanwhile, plunges deeper into insanity, taunting Ricky from behind trailers and appearing out of nowhere, ghostlike, at the roadside. Regardless, the boys focus on their plan to ship the dope to Moncton. They send Trevor and Cory to work the dope field, but the two bail when they remember they have unfinished domestic chores for Sarah.

"Jim Lahey's lost his goddamn mind. I need backup."

The boys head to the field in a stolen courier truck. Ricky is smoking up the truck so badly that Bubbles can't see where he's driving and they crash into Cory and Trevor's car, trapping the pair inside the smouldering wreck. But there's no time to free them—the harvest must continue. The boys hijack an oncoming bus and force its passengers—who just happen to be Rita MacNeil and her band—to work. They start bringing in the weed and break into song to ease their burden.

Once the dope is loaded in the truck, the boys head out—towing Cory and Trevor, still trapped in the car. The tow chain breaks and the pair coast wildly into downtown Dartmouth, unnoticed by the boys. After the boys realize why their load has lightened on the drive into town, they also discover their brakes have been sabotaged and the truck crashes into Cory and Trevor's fresh accident scene. Dope filled courier packages spill everywhere. Solution: call a courier company and have the product shipped properly. And pack Cory and Trevor into one of the boxes to make sure the dope arrives safely.

Just when all seems resolved, Jim Lahey appears in a dress, sporting pistols and strapped with explosives. He points a gun right at Ricky's head, and the street quickly fills with cops, the SWAT team and TV cameras. One overzealous reporter tries to interview Ricky, who tells her to "fuck off." Lahey means business and fires into the air, but Ricky still takes a moment to sign the shipping manifest for the dope.

When the SWAT team attempts to shoot the gun from Lahey's hand, they hit Ricky by mistake. Officer George Green has sent for Randy and he arrives just in time to end the standoff. Still, it's off to psychiatric care for Mr. Lahey, and Ricky, Julian and Bubbles head to jail. Cory and Trevor deliver the goods, and, in an unprecedented act of rebellion, keep the dope money.

rare photo

Bringin' in the weed,
bringin' in the weed,
we shall come rejoicing,
bringin' in the weed.

A good disguise can fool anyone.

RICKYISMS

"The hot tub saved me, it must be fire retarded."
—Yup

"I'm not trying to be mean, I'm just stretched out."
—Ricky sort of apologizing for enslaving Rita MacNeil and her band during weed harvest

"It's not my fault they got off their leeches."
—Aren't leeches hard to get off?

Looks like Cory and Trevor fucked up again.

Mr. Lahey was drunk for the entire season. He's completely fucked.

Hijacking Rita MacNeil's tour bus to make her band harvest weed.

Shipping dope, armed standoffs, SWAT team shooting Ricky, burning vehicles.

SEASON 4
EPISODE XMAS SPECIAL

Bah Humbug Bubbles, and one fuckin' miserable elf.

nomesayin

Lucy's Christmas List
. . . or rather, her Christmas demands:

1. Ricky not showing up drunk for Christmas dinner.

2. Filling her and Sarah's furnace tank with oil.

3. At least seven presents for Trinity.

4. A fur coat.

Title: DEAR SANTA CLAUS GO FUCK YOURSELF
Air Date: DECEMBER 12, 2004

Writers: Mike Clattenburg, Barrie Dunn, Iain MacLeod, Mike Smith, Jonathan Torrens, John Paul Tremblay, Michael Volpe, Robb Wells
Director: Mike Clattenburg
Guest Stars: Paul LeBlanc (Prison Guard), Daniel Lilford (Tree Lot Worker), Paul MacLeod (Minister), Craig Wood (Tree Lot Owner), Stan Carew (Police Officer)

The Sunnyvale Christmas clock is rewound several years for thi hour-long holiday special. Bubbles just can't get into the yuletid spirit this year because everybody seems so stressed out. To mak matters worse, he looks under his bed and spies the last Christma gift his parents, who disappeared long ago, ever gave to him. Th sight of it profoundly saddens him, as he promised himself that h wouldn't open the gift until he was with his family again. Nearby, i Julian's trailer, Lucy gives Julian a mistletoe belt buckle, making hir very uncomfortable. "You're supposed to smooch under the mistletoe Bubbles comments to the camera, "so it's not too difficult to figure ou what she's trying to say." To get away from Lucy, Julian devises a pla to bail Ricky out of jail, thereby killing two birds with one stone: Rick can help with holiday criminal activity (Christmas gift re-marketing and get the amorous Lucy off his back.

"You know that Santa and God aren't the same guy, right?"

Bubbles drives to the jail to collect Ricky and finds him outrage that Julian has interrupted his twelve days of Christmas partying Once in the car, Ricky confides, "Bubbles, I don't know what dad are supposed to do at Christmas. Do you think I'll be able to ge hold of Santa Claus and deal with all this shit?" When they arriv back at the park, Ricky immediately clashes with Jim and Bar Lahey, who are still a couple. Barb threatens her husband with booze-free Christmas if he can't keep his nasty feelings toward Ricky in check.

Ricky finds Julian and tells him how pissed he is about being baile out. Julian brushes it off and tells him about his plan to steal present and Christmas trees and sell them in the park. Bubbles strongl objects. Ricky then visits Lucy but meets with a lukewarm receptior Dejected and confused, he heads over to his dad's place, joined by very melancholy Bubbles. Ray offers his son a bucket-sized glass booze and grills him about manhood, fatherhood and spirituality Completely overwhelmed, Ricky can only assure his father that h has the situation under control: "I'm sending a letter to the big guy Bubbles, now looking even more confused than Ricky, says, "'The bi guy'? That's God, Ricky." "Yeah, God. That's what I said. Santa." Sadl

rare photo
Jamie and friends jacking gifts with a candy-cane crowbar.

Tidings of comfort and joy? At least Randy looks festive.

"The transmission must be fucked or something."
—Ricky to Bubbles, after crashing into another car while leaving the jail parking lot

"Is the transmission drunk, Ricky? 'Cause you are."
—Bubbles

"Dad? You didn't know that [God and Santa are the same person]? I mean, think about it. How would he get around the world in one night? Of course he's the same guy."
—Ricky

"I don't know, would anyone like to suck my cock?"
—Donny the mystery voice in the park responding to a cop's question about the origins of the stolen Christmas trees

Ricky is more confused than usual. When Ray and Bubbles explain that Santa and God are, in fact, different, Ricky is horrified: "Great. Christmas is fucked."

Meanwhile, Barb is doing charity work for the church around town and stumbles upon Randy dressed as an elf at the King of Donair drive-through. Realizing he's a male prostitute (known in the trade as "Smokey"), she insists he come out of the cold and come home with her. When Smokey enters the Laheys' trailer he's surprised to see Jim: "Simon? Simon, you're married?" Seems like Simon and Smokey (Mr. Lahey and Randy) have met before. It's an uncomfortable moment and, when Barb's out of earshot, Lahey demands Smokey only call him Mr. Lahey from now on.

It doesn't take long for people around the park to recognize Randy from childhood. Old grudges quickly resurface and he squeals to Lahey that the boys are stealing gifts and reselling them inside the park. The cops arrive but can't really pin anything on the boys—despite Ricky tearing the door off a cop car with the green New Yorker (looking more like the Shitmobile we know and love every time he gets behind the wheel).

In her kitchen, Barb catches Jim drinking (and Randy in his underwear) and she begins to suspect something is up between the two of them. Life as Mr. Lahey knows it is starting to unravel, as more than Randy's package is on the verge of being exposed. It's Lahey's excuse to really start pounding the booze. In full-on, drunken Grinch-impersonating-Santa mode, Lahey shuts down all the power at the park. When the boys get back from an unsuccessful Christmas tree-stealing run (as well as the Midnight Mass Ray insisted they all attend), they'll greet Christmas in the dark.

Outside the church, Ricky is doing his best to sell the rest of his dope and is meeting with little success, despite his great sales pitch to members of the congregation as they pass: "I know you people like to smoke dope. The service makes a lot more sense when you're stoned." Inside, Lahey arrives plastered and yelling, Barb demands a divorce and Cory and Trevor give Lucy the gift they stole on Ricky's behalf (an arc welder). She totally freaks. It's the worst Christmas ever. Bubbles gets up and leaves in total disgust with everyone. Ricky, in a rare moment of insight, recognizes that his buddy's departure is absolutely justified and takes over the pulpit

Sunnyvale is glowing with the magical spirit of Christmas and Julian's stolen lights.

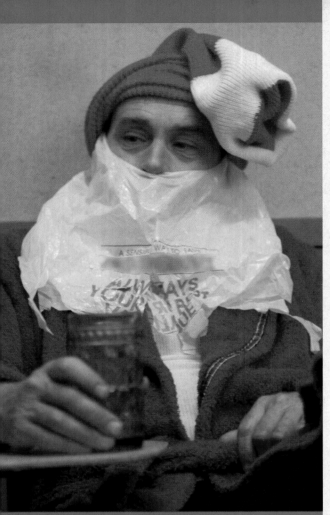

Kris Kringle's sleigh isn't the only thing loaded with holiday cheer.

to give one of the most inspired speeches of his life. We have los the true meaning of Christmas, he says, by worrying about gifts and money and focusing on all the stress of the season. What Christmas is really about is getting drunk and stoned with your family and friends—or if you aren't into booze and dope, at least you should spend time with your family and friends. Linus, with all his preaching to Charlie Brown about Bethlehem and "tidings of great joy," couldn' have said it better.

Later, we find the boys spending Christmas with Bubbles around a bonfire kindled by Lahey's decorations, which they've expropriated and they convince Bubs that he should finally open the gift from his parents because he is with his family now—Ricky and Julian are his family. Bubbles agrees and tears open the package. It's an electric bubble-making machine. He's completely thrilled because, he explains, he was always trying to make bubbles as a kid. More importantly, there is a card from his mom, who explains why she and his dad left when Bubbles was a child. His father had gotten into trouble with organized crime and they worried Bubbles migh be in danger if they stuck around, so they left him in the care o Julian's grandmother. You don't shed a tear here and you're no human. The warmth in our hearts exceeds that of the wooden reindeer-stoked bonfire.

The show ends with Julian's thoughts on the possibility of going to university, Ricky fixing up the Shitmobile as he contemplates getting his grade ten (aiming a little lower) and Bubbles having his firs happy Christmas since he was a kid. God bless us, every one.

RICKYISMS

"You're not fuckin' Santa Claus, Julian, and I don't need your cherry trees."
—Ricky's not in the receiving mood

"A man is supposed to . . . umm . . . always be thinking about stuff . . . about his family and for to make himself do things that are gonna gooder up the family up around and gooder it up."
—Ricky answers Ray on what he learned about being a man while he was in the joint

BAD BOYS SCALE

No shortage of holiday booze with Ricky, buds and guards in jail. And Mr. Lahey goes off the wagon big time.

Everyone gets high at the correctional facility. Ricky sells and distributes hash in and out of the church.

Julian "re-markets" Christmas trees, presents, lights and decorations in a brilliant yuletide scheme. Gunfight at Christmas tree lot.

rare photo
It's a ho-ho-ho-holdup.

RICKY'S
What is Christmas?

"You know . . . I just got out of jail, which was awesome. In jail we don't have presents and lights and trees, we just get stoned and drunk. It's the best time. Now I get out here and I'm all stressed out, my girlfriend breaks up with me and that's not what Christmas should be. It should be people getting drunk and stoned with their friends and family, people that you love. Who here is drunk right now? How many people are drunk besides Julian? [Many hands in the air.] That's so awesome! And dope. God doesn't give a shit if you smoke dope. You're in church, so you can't lie, how many people are stoned right now? [Many hands go up, including the pastor's.] That's what I thought. That's Christmas! None of this presents and lights and stress and shit. It's getting drunk and stoned with friends, family and people you love. And Bubbles, my friend Bubbles, has been trying to teach me what Christmas really is and I wasn't really listening to him, and I was at the mall stealing stuff and everything else, and now I realize he's back at the trailer park by himself right now. I'm going to go back there with him and I'm going to get drunk and stoned with him and everybody in here should do the same thing. Get drunk and stoned with your families. If you don't smoke or drink, just spend time with your families. It's awesome. Merry Christmas. I'm going to get drunk and stoned with my friend Bubbles right now."

TRAILER PARK BOYS
Postcards from the Park

Anyone got a track? 'Cause we got a cover.

Citizen of what country ma'am? How long have you been away? Did you buy or receive any goods?

I'm ready for my close-up now, Mr. DeMille.

That cocksucker's fuckin' deeeeelicious!

What's the alcohol content of motor oil? Watch it, Jim.

SEASON 5

Thanks to Cory and Trevor, the boys' dope money is popping up and out all over the park. Lucy shows off her latest assets.

nomesayin

Julian's jail-time reading is *Triumph of the Salmon* (don't look for it in stores).

On the way to Dennis and Terry's, the boys stop on the side of the road for a pee that lasts longer than Austin Powers's upon emerging from his cryogenic state.

Bubbles tells Dennis and Terry how they synced up *The Dark Side of the Moon* with *The Wizard of Oz* while in jail. (Almost worth going to jail for…)

Title: GIVE PEACE A CHANCE
Air Date: APRIL 17, 2005

Writers: Mike Clattenburg, John Paul Tremblay, Robb Wells, Mike Smith, Jonathan Torrens
Director: Mike Clattenburg
Guest Stars: Bernard Robichaud (Cyrus), Richard Collins (Paul Collins), James Swansburg (Officer Ted Johnston), Fukuko Saito (Dennis and Terry's Grandmother), Novalea Buchan (Police Officer), Nobu Adilman (Dennis), Mio Adilman (Terry)

"Jail sucks," laments Julian. "Been here too many times, the thrill is gone." Besides, a life of affluence awaits the boys upon their release. A stretch limo even greets them at the jail gates. Inside the luxury ride, they toast Cory and Trevor, who should have secured the boys' fortune with the massive dope deal at the end of last season. What they don't know is that Cory and Trevor, fucked up big time. They squandered the money and Barb duped them out of buying the park with her phony agreement (a car lease). Still riding high on the false hopes of park ownership—"I own a trailer park now. I don't need any keys," enthuses Ricky—the boys stop by Dennis and Terry's grandmother's home to score some dope. Bubbles is uncomfortable because Dennis and Terry—appearing for the first time in the show— tend to walk around in bathrobes with "their birds hanging out."

"The first thing I'm going to do, I'm going to kill Jim Lahey."

The boys couldn't have arrived at a worse time. Dennis and Terry are about to do a big deal and a limo parked out front is bound to draw unwelcome attention. Their business associate shows up and it's none other than Cyrus. The guns come out and the fuck-offs start flying, spooking the limo driver, who leaves the boys to find their way home by cab. When Julian finds an empty box under his trailer and realizes their weed fortune is gone, they bail on the cab.

Ray fills the boys in on Cory and Trevor's betrayal. Ricky storms out of the trailer, gun in hand, looking for revenge. He's sidetracked by a reunion with Trinity and Lucy, during which Sarah tries to tell him to stay away from Cory and Trevor. Speaking of whom, they're hanging out at J-Roc's joint when Ricky pulls up. They bolt inside and Ricky comes after them like a crazed grizzly. The whole park seems to show up along with the cops, who inform Ricky of a peace bond that ensures he stays 50 feet away from the inept pair.

Of course, there's still Lahey to deal with. Ricky corners him, but Lahey stops him cold with a heartfelt apology; he's also clean and sober. Ricky considers shaking Lahey's hand, but Julian interrupts. He's not buying it, and Ricky, coming to his senses, storms off.

rare photo

Bubbles's inability to serve or volley doesn't seem to diminish his love for the game.

The boys will be leaving jail in style; a stretch "lemonzine" awaits.

RICKYISMS

"Bagminton really sucks but Bubbles loves it."
—Ricky, passing time in jail

Ricky, listening to Lahey's rehab-and-recovery sob story, offers to play him a song on the **"magdolin."**

Entrusting all the dope money to Trevor and Cory for safekeeping until they return from jail might not have been the boys' brightest idea.

BAD BOYS SCALE

 The odd drink in Julian's hand. Lahey claims to be sober.

 Dennis and Terry fix Ricky up.

 The number of guns drawn between Cyrus and the boys is truly inspired. You would have to tune into *Cops* to find better gun action.

Title: THE SHIT PUPPETS
Air Date: APRIL 24, 2005

Writers: Mike Clattenburg, John Paul Tremblay, Robb Wells, Mike Smith, Jonathan Torrens
Director: Mike Clattenburg
Guest Stars: Bernard Robichaud (Cyrus), Richard Collins (Phil Collins), Fukuko Saito (Dennis and Terry's Grandmother), Nobu Adilman (Dennis), Mio Adilman (Terry)

Life in Sunnyvale can mean a meager existence, and if you're Ricky, sleeping on the ground and using a take-out container as a pillow— well, sometimes it just plain sucks. Julian's up early, however, determined to improve his life. He goes to pick up Cory and Trevor, but Sarah doesn't loan them out easily: "No chips off the floor of the car. You gotta feed them. And if you're gonna leave them, crack a window and give them water."

"Where you getting the dope? Going to the Floppy Bird Brothers?"

J-Roc has been stealing groceries from the supermarket grocery pickup and reselling them back at the park. It's a living, but it hardly explains the state-of-the-art recording equipment in his trailer. Turns out Cory and Trevor gave him nine grand to let them cut a track on his CD. Ricky, now wide awake, confronts J-Roc and T about the gear. They say the money's from GST cheques, a lemonade stand, flea markets, half-price hot shit, returning bottles, saving money, even finding it in a ditch. Ricky grabs the machines, one of which squeals "J-Roc baby," breaks records and takes their washing machine.

He gives the sound gear to Trinity, hoping to make amends with Lucy. Ricky can't figure out why he's been attracted to Lucy since returning from jail, but Bubbles can. Seems the dope money bought Lucy fake boobs, of which Bubbles proudly calculates one-third ownership.

Julian, Cory and Trevor head to Dennis and Terry's. Disguised, they sneak in with shotguns and steal two huge hockey bags of hash. Meanwhile, Ricky decides he'll start growing dope again to impress Lucy and heads over to the same place to buy supplies. Worried, Bubbles tails Ricky in his go-kart. Ricky sees Julian, Cory and Trevor running out of the house and speeding off. Moments later, Dennis, Terry and Cyrus storm out with guns firing. Ricky bolts and Bubbles executes about a 4G U-turn to follow. Back at the park, Bubbles tells Julian that their cover was likely blown when Cyrus spotted him. Cyrus makes a positive ID by claiming to be ripped off by the "Hubba Bubbles gang."

Cyrus and his boys show up, guns blazing, but Lahey has already summoned the cops, who quickly defuse the situation. Julian cleverly reveals a package of hash that mysteriously has landed in his lap. Terry shouts "Hey, that's our hash," thus confessing their guilt. The remaining hash haul is huge and needs to be hidden in a place where nobody will find it, right in plain sight.

Looks like Ricky's return policy for J-Roc's dope-funded recording gear.

nomesayin

MR. LAHEY'S SHIT ANALOGIES

Lahey, very cryptically, begins to refer to the boys as "shit puppets." What's he up to?

TRAILER PARK TIPS

Persistence is a great quality in life, and there are none more persistent than Ricky. While taking back the DJ gear from J-Roc, for some reason (known only to the darkest crevices of Ricky's mind) he also decides to take the washing machine. Getting this appliance out of the front door is hard enough, but loading it into a shopping cart proves to be a real bastard. After three failed tries, he just leaves the fucker in the road. The most important part of persistence is knowing when to give up.

rare photo
Dennis and Terry's grandmother, the cookie pusher. The cookies don't fall too far from the tree.

Sarah allows Julian to take Cory and Trevor.

BEST LINES

"Stand by the stick and stay."
—Julian throws a stick into the distance for Cory and Trevor so they don't overhear his conversation with Ricky

"What's wrong with parents these days?"
—Mr. Lahey after surviving a brutal Bottle Kids attack

RICKYISM

Ricky refers to Cory and Trevor as

"Simple and Garfuckal"

◀ J-Roc-rhyme-shakin', porn-makin', grocery-takin' badass.

BAD BOYS SCALE

Lahey still not drinking.

The boys score enough dope to . . . to . . . to pave a driveway!

That prick Cyrus insures the gunfire count is outta the park.

Title: THE FUCKIN' WAY SHE GOES
Air Date: MAY 1, 2005

Writers: Mike Clattenburg, John Paul Tremblay, Robb Wells, Mike Smith, Jonathan Torrens
Director: Mike Clattenburg
Guest Stars: James Swansburg (Officer Ted Johnston)

"The Fuckin' Way She Goes" begins with Bubbles and Ricky busily heating up their massive hash score on a BBQ so they can pave Ray's driveway with it. "It's Julian's plan and I do trust his judgmental," worries Ricky, "but it seems a little fucked to me." He then adds, "I am not going to put my dad into jeopardization with a hash driveway in his yard." Bubbles assesses the idea as "Very low risk, until you get caught." The boys fall out over this strategy and Julian (who thinks Cory and Trevor are doing a good job) fires Ricky, who can't quite believe what he's hearing: "You're going to fire me after I raised Cory and Trevor?"

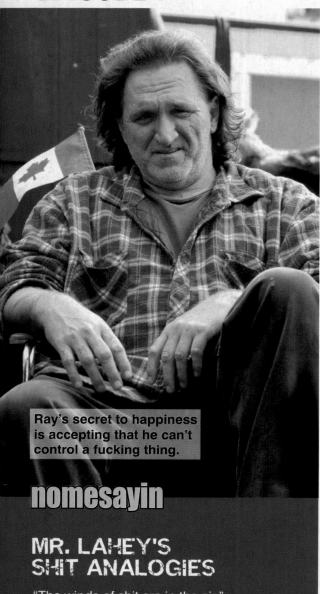

Ray's secret to happiness is accepting that he can't control a fucking thing.

nomesayin

"I'm not the kinda person to say I toadaso, but you know what? I TOADASO! I FUCKIN' TOADASO!"

After patching up their differences, Ricky convinces Julian to take Ray out for a night on the town so Ricky can BBQ a nice dinner for Lucy and Trinity. If he only had food and his own BBQ, this plan might just win Lucy over. He offers to give J-Roc back some of the DJ equipment in exchange for food and a grill. J-Roc, already making some serious scril by jacking food from the "grocery bitches," is happy to provide for Ricky and the cookout is a go.

Julian takes Ray, Bubs, Cory and Trevor down to the strip bar to watch some modern dance. Watching all the naked women gets a rise out of Cory and Trevor, much to the disgust of the dancers and the other customers. To make matters worse, and because things always get worse, it looks as though an unrepentant Ray has blown all the drinking money on video lottery terminals at the back of the bar—"That's the way she goes, boys." Julian, seeing that things are declining rapidly, packs up the crew and heads for home. There, they find the fire department putting out Ray's trailer, which looks slightly less devastated than Halifax after the 1917 explosion.

Looks like somebody forgot he was cooking French fries on Ray's stove and left with Lucy to go for a romantic bang in the back seat of the Shitmobile behind the muffler shop. That's one less trailer for the boys to crash in. The way she goes, boys, the fuckin' way she goes.

MR. LAHEY'S SHIT ANALOGIES

"The winds of shit are in the air."
—Lahey picking up a shit vibe

TRAILER PARK TIPS

Don't entrust Ray with your liquor money when he's in the middle of a raging VLT addiction. You won't get your rum and cola or lap dance; you won't even get a glass of water. It's just common sense, boys.

rare photo
Nothing like the flames of a small BBQ fire to kindle the spirit of friendship.

Nothing but smoke, where Ray's trailer used to be.

RICKYISM

"I cannot work with those fuckin' dicks, so I am going to give you an ultimariam right now: it's either me or Gumby and Perfuckio."
—Ricky to Julian about working with Cory and Trevor

Unfortunately, Ray's chair had to ride in the trunk because there was no room in the back seat.

BAD BOYS SCALE

More suspected drinking from Lahey, but nothing confirmed.

The hash driveway is a perfect example of human ingenuity—unless you want to drive on it.

There must be something criminal about a driveway made of hash.

135

SEASON 5 EPISODE 4

Title: YOU GOT TO BLAME THE THING UP THERE
Air Date: MAY 8, 2005

Writers: Mike Clattenburg, John Paul Tremblay, Robb Wells, Mike Smith, Jonathan Torrens
Director: Mike Clattenburg
Guest Stars: Jacob Rolfe (Jacob), Richard Collins (Phil Collins)

Ray's trailer fire has left pretty much everybody homeless. Bubble feels terrible because he's convinced he caused it, though Ray simpl can't figure him for it. Julian decides to help Ray out by taking Cor and Trevor to rip off gumball machines for the change ("You ca have some gum only after we get the money!"), then cash out th VLTs down at the strip bar. After successfully stealing about 10 pounds of coins, they head to the hardware store and "LC" (Nov Scotia Liquor Corporation) to set Ray up with a tent, some utensil and lots of booze.

"You lied to the guy in the chair."

Ricky and Bubbles are doing their part for Ray, too. They musc in on J-Roc's grocery-stealing business, and he isn't too please about it. Things come to a head back in the park when Ricky—in moment that would make Scarface step back and say "Holy shit!"-shoots up J-Roc's basket of food at point-blank range. (Try to imagin Tony Montana staring down a bag of groceries: "Say hello to my littl friend." J-Roc retreats, but not until insult is added to injury when h endures a Bottle Kids attack of impressive savagery.

Things start to look up for Ray when Ricky successfully retrieve Ray's old Western Star sleeper cab from the dump with the he of Bubbles's friend Shitty Bill ("Pooped himself when he was little guy. Name kinda stuck.") Ray's thrilled; it's home, sweet hom Things seem to be wrapping up nicely when Lucy lets it slip th Ricky, not Bubbles, caused the fire. Bubbles is devastated and make clear to Ricky, in no uncertain terms, "We're done. No more hugs."

Ricky tries to explain: "I got back here and the place was golfing flames—there was nothing I could do, buddy. Yeah, like flames fucki golfin', golfin', golfin' out the roof and the fuckin' door. There wa nothing I could do." And as if this hole isn't deep enough, Ricky dig some more. "You started takin' the blame," he says to Bubbles, "and mean I didn't want you to but you did. You're my best friend so I got let you. That's what best friends do."

Julian takes Ricky aside and tells him he has a lot of making up to d It isn't pretty.

Ricky confesses that he, and not Bubbles, burned down Ray's trailer. Kind of a low point in their relationship.

nomesayin

Always in search of a good laugh, Trinity writes the words "Bum head" on Julian's forehead while he's asleep; she punctuates this by drawing a kitten on each one of his cheeks. It should be noted that few people —only someone as sweet as Trinity, or, maybe, kitty-crazy Bubbles—would survive such a risky form of arts and crafts.

rare photo
Ricky and Bubbles stealing groceries for Ray. Fuck buying them from J-Roc.

Ricky tries to look on the bright side. Unfortunately, it's covered in soot.

RICKYISM

"I was planning on taking the blame because there was a pretty good chance that I did it—well, I mean, I DID do it. But Bubbles took the blame and once someone takes the blame, what do you do? I couldn't take it then. He'd already taken it."

—Ricky's understanding of the whole business of blame is fascinating, and almost plausible

◄ The thinker?
I think not.

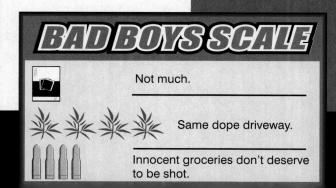

BAD BOYS SCALE

Not much.

Same dope driveway.

Innocent groceries don't deserve to be shot.

SEASON 5 EPISODE 5

Commander Bubbles is ready to launch this cocksucker.

nomesayin

MR. LAHEY'S SHIT ANALOGIES

"Goddamn shit apple driving a Shitmobile. What kind of father lets his daughter do that?"

"You just opened Pandora's shit box, Ray."

Title: JIM LAHEY IS A FUCKIN' DRUNK AND HE ALWAYS WILL BE
Air Date: MAY 15, 2005

Writers: Mike Clattenburg, John Paul Tremblay, Robb Wells, Mike Smith, Jonathan Torrens, Iain MacLeod
Director: Mike Clattenburg
Guest Stars: Richard Collins (Phil Collins), Iain MacLeod (Head Mall Cop)

The show begins with Randy and Phil Collins wedged very, very, very very tightly into kayaks, practising their paddling technique for an upcoming trip. Unfortunately, Randy decides he can't go because he's worried about Mr. Lahey hitting the bottle again. It's a peaceful scene—two round and jolly fellows discussing the great outdoors, as well as the benefits of hypnosis tapes for people with addiction issues (related to booze . . . no mention of cheeseburgers). It's peaceful alright, until they're hit with the largest fuckin' bottle attack in history. Trapped in the kayaks, they're sitting ducks and the Bottle Kids exact a terrible toll on the easiest targets they have ever had the pleasure of firing upon. Randy's threat to "friggin' tell on them" goes unheeded.

"I have God to thank for everything."

Park relations have been very tense since Ray's trailer burned down and Ricky is trying to make it up to both Ray and Bubbles. The only person who seems happy is Trinity, who's been driving the Shitmobile around the park. The boys decide to cheer up Bubs by taking him to buy a "bagminton" set, but Bubbles spies a model rocket kit at the department store and Ricky decides to get it for him. Using an ingenious fraudulent-cheque-writing system, he steals the rocket, the boys get caught, and Cory and Trevor take the blame (that's why it's ingenious).

Back at the park, they prepare for launch. Bubbles hasn't been this excited since performing in *From Russia With the Love Bone*. Seeing Bubbles's flight suit and a very cool tinfoil-covered helmet, casual passersby could be excused for thinking they were looking at Chuck Yeager. Ricky and Julian, however, still look like Ricky and Julian wearing old helmets covered in tinfoil (this is thought to be the only instance, ever, when Julian is caught wearing something that fails to match with black). Ricky can't get into the spirit of the "Naysa" jargon that Bubbles encourages, but the launch proceeds. Needless to say it's friggin' decent!

Of course, Lahey ruins the mood (by running over the rocket when it parachutes back to earth), but Ray catches him drinking. As it happens, Lahey's been guzzling vodka out of water bottles since he first set foot out of the mental hospital. Julian was right all along. But Jim has a plan. Apparently the liquor makes him see everything more clearly. Does it now Jim?

rare photo
Nobody gets more out of a chequebook than Ricky.

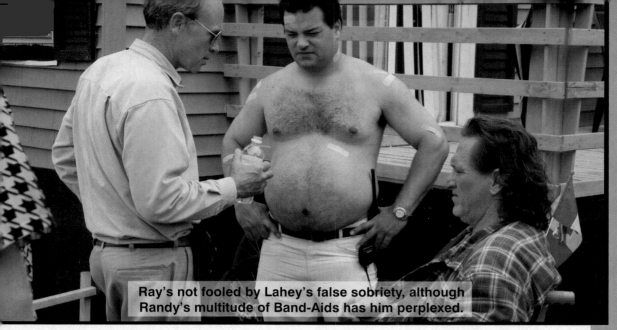

Ray's not fooled by Lahey's false sobriety, although Randy's multitude of Band-Aids has him perplexed.

RICKYISMS

When Ricky says "worst case scenario" somehow his brain twists and turns it into
"Worse case Ontario."

The rocket kit includes **"decnals"** to stick on the rocket's exterior.

◄ Boldly going. . .

Lahey is back. Back with a vengeance.

Minor "space weed" reference.

A stolen rocket that made Bubbles so happy, the theft shouldn't be considered a crime.

SEASON 5 EPISODE 6

Tough times at Sunnyvale. The glass is neither half full nor half empty. It's just empty.

nomesayin

MR. LAHEY'S SHIT ANALOGIES

"Shit moths, Randy. Shit moths. They started off as tiny little shit larvae, Randy, and then they grew into shitapillars, a pandemic of shitapillars everywhere you look, Randy. Shitapillars." . . .

And if you didn't believe him the first time:

"They almost drove me over the goddamned edge, boy. Tried to exterminate them, I tried to put an end to the shitapillars' life cycle, but I failed and now, shit moths, Randy. Every fuckin' one of them, shit moths."

"Randy, sometimes it's a lot better to watch a shit tree grow than to try and shake the shit fruit out of it."

140

Title: DON'T CROSS THE SHIT LINE
Air Date: MAY 22, 2005

Writers: Mike Clattenburg, John Paul Tremblay, Robb Wells, Mike Smith, Jonathan Torrens, Iain MacLeod
Director: Mike Clattenburg
Guest Stars: Jacob Rolfe (Jacob), James Swansburg (Officer Ted Johnston), George Green (Officer George Green)

Things are getting pretty grim for the boys. Ricky and Julian are a each other's throats, Bubbles is slowly starving and Ray is dying o thirst (he even tries to steal Julian's rum and cola—like trying to take raw meat from a tiger). To top it off, Lahey is pissed that Ray ratted hir out for drinking again and decides to exterminate the boys like "shitapillars." He begins by sending Randy over to Ray's with ar eviction notice—but this is of little concern to Ray, who's too focusec on finding liquor. J-Roc comes to his rescue by offering booze anc stolen groceries if he and Bubbles will "act" in his latest erotic masterpiece, *Greasy Trailer Park Girls Gone Wild*.

"No one wants to admit that they ate nine cans of Ravioli, but I did, and I'm ashamed of myself."

J-Roc commits to making a "real" film this time; he dispenses with plo and character development altogether and uses a more penetrating approach to cinematic storytelling. The ensemble cast includes ar appearance by Lucy, and Ricky's not impressed. Filming begins without Lucy, who doesn't realize that punctuality is just as importan to a pornographer as is the money shot, but the other ladies make up for her absence with inspired performances. J-Roc directs them to dance for the disabled Ray and use their erotic healing power to help him get up from the prison of his wheelchair. Although light on story this production spares no expense in the special effects department a smoke machine and bubble-maker (operated by you-know-who provide a sophisticated, almost lavish backdrop.

Needless to say, Lahey has not been standing around, watching the world go by. His mind has been working triple overtime, producing a shit avalanche of shit analogies as he conducts his crazed surveillance of the day's illegal activities—not to mention his ongoing project o stealing the boys' liquor and subsequent crazy-assed labelling of the bottles with the owners' names.

Not only does Lahey manage to get J-Roc busted for grocery theft, he also captures Ray on tape standing up from his chair and walking— strange as this may sound, walking's forbidden if you happen to be collecting long-term disability money from the government. Ray soon finds himself in jail on a rap for disability fraud. Thanks there, Jimmy.

rare photo
Lahey-mixin' drinks and stirrin' up shit.

On the set of *Greasy Trailer Park Girls Gone Wild*.

Strike 3 for Bubbles

Just a brief word about Bubbles and the porn business. With three J-Roc productions under his belt (so to speak), he is precisely 0 for 3 when it comes to actually hooking up with any of the lovely ladies who populate the cinematic works. Unquestionably, Bubbles finds the business "greasy," but it sure would be nice if he got his game on at least once. Poor, frisky Bubbles. We feel your pain, bud.

The boys will have to discount any hash that tastes like feet.

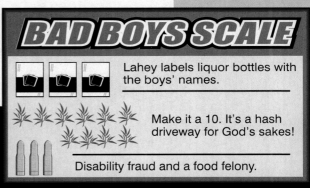

BAD BOYS SCALE

Lahey labels liquor bottles with the boys' names.

Make it a 10. It's a hash driveway for God's sakes!

Disability fraud and a food felony.

141

Title: THE WINDS OF SHIT
Air Date: MAY 29, 2005

Writers: Mike Clattenburg, John Paul Tremblay, Robb Wells, Mike Smith, Jonathan Torrens
Director: Mike Clattenburg
Guest Stars: Collen Zimmerman (Student), Daniel O'Leary (Registrar), Chase Duffy (Police Officer)

That bastard Lahey is upping the ante again: he's planning to put Julian's grandmother's trailer on the market to force Julian's hand. He figures Julian will have to break the law to raise the money to buy his place back—and Lahey will be there to catch him.

Meanwhile, Ricky has visited Ray in jail, and the old man hates it on the inside. Ricky vows to raise bail money and wants to start cashing in on the hash driveway. Julian, however, wants to sell the hash with as little risk as possible, so he sends Ricky to attend vocational school and sell the drugs to the students. As always, Bubbles gets right to the heart of things: "There's two ways to look at it, really. You either go to school to learn or you go to school to sell drugs." Full classrooms stop Ricky from enrolling (phew!), so he bribes a counsellor—with hash—for a gig as a janitor.

Off to school.

nomesayin

MR. LAHEY'S SHIT ANALOGIES

"You know what a shit barometer is, Bubbles?"
—Lahey
"No."—Bubbles
"It measures shit pressure in the air, you can feel it. Listen Bubbles . . . hear that? The sounds of the whispering winds of shit. Can you hear it?"—Lahey
"No."—Bubbles, becoming more spooked by the second
"Oh, but you will, my sorry little friend, when the old shit barometer rises. And you'll feel it, too. Your ears will implode from the shit pressure. You were warned, Bubs, but you picked the wrong side. Beware, my friend, shit winds are a' comin'."

"Who taught Trinity to drive? Not Lucy, me."

Julian's plan is simple. Ricky takes orders at school during the day, and the boys return at night to leave hash in lockers and collect payment (Ricky uses the "honourly system"). As they are readying themselves for the night's transactions, Lahey drops by and delivers a disturbing speech about how the "shit winds are a' coming." It's enough to scare Buffy the Vampire Slayer, never mind Bubbles. Later on in the dark, drafty school, as they go from locker to locker, the boys all seem a little spooked by Jim's slurred, prophetic words.

Pausing to take a leak, Ricky hears the eerie "shit-wind ghosts" and is so freaked he opens fire on a defenseless urinal. Chaos erupts and the boys beat a hasty retreat from the school, only to be stopped by the cops in the parking lot. Ricky brilliantly talks the boys out of this jam by telling the cops he thought he saw kids around the school and came to investigate himself. Bubbles is in particular awe as they head home. Next morning, after a refreshing night's sleep in the Shitmobile, Julian tells Ricky that Ray wants to stay in jail a little longer (a lie—Julian needs the bail money to buy back his trailer). Lahey outs Ricky as a janitor, and not a student, but Lucy takes more interest in the sincerity of Ricky's effort to be a provider.

Looks like the winds of shit have been downgraded from hurricane status—for now.

rare photo
Lucy and Ricky are hitting it off now that his janitor and hash-selling jobs at the school are going so well.

The janitor job would be okay except for all the trash.

RICKYISMS

"I tried to go to school and get my book thinkin' and learnin' and stuff more brainly in my head, and I can't force CB or tell you what I'm trying to say here 'cause my brain is scrambly."

-Ricky trying really, really hard to explain something to Trinity

"A lot of people might say I'm stupid. I don't know. I don't think I am. Like, I'm probably smarter than that [holding up a plastic plant]. This thing here [holding up a clock] is smarter than me, I guess, 'cause it has a battery."

-Ricky, assessing his academic potential for the school guidance counsellor

◄ Lahey's selling Julian's grandmother's trailer to raise money to spring Cyrus from jail. It's a plot inspired by more booze than any human should look at, let alone drink.

BEST LINES

"What are you doing? You reading books again?"
—Ray

"What's wrong with reading books?"
—Julian

"Nothing wrong with reading books. But there's only one book that counts, Julian, and it's the Bible. It says to help your friends."
—Ray

"Does it say anything about you ripping off insurance companies, pretending you're in a wheelchair and getting caught drunk, dancing with hos, making porn flicks? Huh? Anything in your book about that, Ray?"
—Julian

"It's open to interpretation, Julian, it's the Bible."
—Ray

BAD BOYS SCALE

Lahey's "winds of shit" speech warrants a perfect score.

Selling hash at school also deserves a perfect score.

Ricky's unprovoked assault on a high-school urinal knows no precedent.

Title: DRESSED ALL OVER & ZESTY MORDANT
Air Date: JUNE 5, 2005

Writers: Mike Clattenburg, John Paul Tremblay, Robb Wells, Mike Smith, Jonathan Torrens
Director: Mike Clattenburg
Guest Stars: James Swansburg (Officer Ted Johnston), George Green (Officer George Green), Kim Dunn (Mall Security Gary)

A responsible Ricky ensures the Shitmobile is in good running order before letting Trinity drive.

nomesayin

MR. LAHEY'S SHIT ANALOGIES

"From a distance they look like ordinary flowers, Randy, but when you get right down and stick your nose in you realize they're shit flowers. And there's a whole bouquet there, right in front of Ray's trailer."

Julian has a plan that can't fail (really, this one is foolproof . . . provided no fools are involved). They're going to distribute driveway hash all over the province inside hollowed-out shopping cart handles. The problem is they need two hundred carts and Gary the mall cop hasn't been that cooperative of late—in fact, he really hates it when Bubbles steals his precious carts.

Julian persuades a reluctant Bubs to go to the mall again by appealing to his vanity: "Who's the king of the carts?" Knowing damn well who is, Bubbles agrees. Unfortunately, the ever-vigilant Gary catches him and sends him packing—but not before he updates Bubbles on how terrible life really is as a mall cop.

"Watch out Ricky, his pants are off!"

When Bubbles returns empty-handed, Julian pays a visit to the mall and manages to convince Gary to supply many, many shopping carts using nothing more than his considerable charm, debating skills and a big fuckin' gun aimed right at Gary's mangy head. Bubbles' triumphant return to the park in his go-kart, hauling a dozen shopping buggies like an Australian road train, is a wondrous sight to behold.

Meanwhile, Trinity is hanging with Ricky because Lucy and Sarah have gone off to get drunk, and she asks her dad if she can take the car to the store. Being the generous father that he is, Ricky agrees, but only if she drives responsibly and remembers to lock all three doors. Off Trinity goes—the trunk loaded with 12 pounds of hash.

Needless to say, a preteen girl driving a three-doored New Yorker quickly catches the eye of the local constabulary. They impound the car and charge Trinity with everything short of war crimes. Ricky, for his part, thinks jail might be a good life lesson for a nine-year-old and Lucy, for her part, offers to bang the arresting officer if he'll let Trinity off, which gets her thrown in jail too.

rare photo
It's a proud moment when your kid gets behind the wheel and ventures out on her own, or goes to the store for some chips.

Every company could use a shrewd negotiator like Julian. Here he arranges to increase the supply of discarded carts available for Bubbles.

RICKYISMS

"You know your thoughts might be better than mine, but I have thoughts going around in my head about different thinkings and brain things you can use, and doing different things, and I think I know what's best for my daughter."
—Father knows best

"What Lucy doesn't know won't learn her."
—Makes perfect sense

Trinity does not go quietly into that good night. Armed with a bottle, she does what she can to resist arrest for driving without a licence. One day she'll learn her dad's police-negotiation skills. One day.

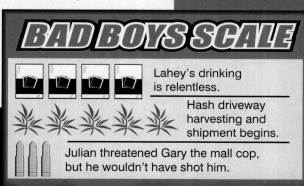

BAD BOYS SCALE

Lahey's drinking is relentless.

Hash driveway harvesting and shipment begins.

Julian threatened Gary the mall cop, but he wouldn't have shot him.

Title: I AM THE LIQUOR
Air Date: JUNE 12, 2005

Writers: Mike Clattenburg, John Paul Tremblay, Robb Wells, Mike Smith, Jonathan Torrens, Iain MacLeod
Director: Mike Clattenburg
Guest Stars: Bernard Robichaud (Cyrus), Nobu Adilman (Dennis), Mio Adilman (Terry)

Realizing his car is impounded—along with his entire family—Ricky opts to jog to the courthouse to collect Lucy and Trinity, but gives up after about 5 meters. In desperation he commandeers Bub's go-kart, which is just as well, as he's been experiencing chest pain lately. Bubbles isn't pleased that Ricky is using it, knowing he'll run it into curbs and do burn-outs and doughnuts non-stop. Our nearsighted friend's day becomes even worse when Julian needs him to go tell Ray he's not getting out of prison yet because Julian needs all the bail money to buy his trailer back from Lahey. But first they're going to the impound lot to retrieve the hash from the Shitmobile's trunk. When Julian whistles for Cory and Trevor to come and guard the driveway, Bubbles realizes for the first time that Julian actually treats them like two dogs. He doesn't approve.

"Holy fuck, my whole family's in jail. I better go get them out!"

Across town, Ricky slides Bubbles's go-kart into a curb in front of the courthouse. Ricky jumps out, sparks up a quick one to calm his nerves, and goes inside to confront the legal system. He then gives the presiding judge an impassioned speech about the nature of family, fatherhood and homelessness, plus the dangers of mixing weed with booze. Somehow this manages to secure the release of his girlfriend and daughter.

Back at the park, Lahey tricks Trevor into revealing that Ray's driveway is paved with hash. Then Lahey heads over and uses the $7,500 Julian has put down on his grandmother's trailer to spring Cyrus, Dennis and Terry from jail. While Jim is doing this, the boys are having a collective meltdown: Ricky finds out what Julian did with Ray's bail money and angrily declares their friendship over; Bubbles can no longer stand the tension; he insists Julian apologize to Ricky because he knows that Julian has, in a rare occurrence, fucked over his friend for his own personal gain. They are all family, he reminds them, and must stick together.

This last point is particularly apt since right about now the other residents of the park begin fleeing like rats leaving a sinking ship: word is out that Cyrus and friends are heading Sunnyvale way, and they're looking for payback.

Bubbles practises Sunnyvale diplomacy.

nomesayin

MR. LAHEY'S SHIT ANALOGIES

"Instead of working against all the horseshit that goes on in this park, I'm going to encourage it. And then I'm going to let those little shitty-shit board members and their sexy mayor, Julian, destroy themselves, Randy."

"We are going to need a few more shit puppets for our play, Randy, and they've got to be angry shit puppets—and you've got to make them angry. You say whatever it takes to make them angry but they're not angry at us, Randy. Shit puppets are supposed to be angry at other shit puppets."

rare photo

Bubbles, disguised as a cedar, attempts to contact Ray without drawing any attention to himself.

Julian keeps Ray's bail money, intending to buy his trailer back from Lahey.

RICKYISMS

"Julian starts feeding me bullshit that I don't have assurance on my car—I don't have assurance on my car!"
—Ricky pissed that Julian won't let him drive his car

"I am the liquor." In case you didn't already know.

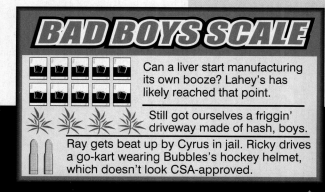

BAD BOYS SCALE

Can a liver start manufacturing its own booze? Lahey's has likely reached that point.

Still got ourselves a friggin' driveway made of hash, boys.

Ray gets beat up by Cyrus in jail. Ricky drives a go-kart wearing Bubbles's hockey helmet, which doesn't look CSA-approved.

Ricky cheats the Grim Reaper, thanks to a brain that runs on minimal energy.

nomesayin

MR. LAHEY'S SHIT ANALOGIES

"Feel that?"—Lahey
"Feel what, Mr. Lahey?"—Randy
"The way the shit clings to the air."
"Shit clings to the air?"
"It's already started, my dear good friend."
"What's started, Mr. Lahey?"
"The shit blizzard."

Why We Love Bubbles:

"I'll tell you right now I am fuckin' dead against gunfights, I hate getting in 'em. Ricky and Julian, I don't think they realize just how fuckin' dangerous they are."

Title: SHIT BLIZZARD
Air Date: JUNE 19, 2005

Writers: Mike Clattenburg, John Paul Tremblay, Robb Wells, Mike Smith, Jonathan Torrens
Director: Mike Clattenburg
Guest Stars: James Swansburg (Officer Ted Johnston), George Green (Officer George Green), Bernard Robichaud (Cyrus), Richard Collins (Phil Collins), Fukuko Saito (Dennis and Terry's Grandmother), Novalea Buchan (Police Officer), Nobu Adilman (Dennis), Mio Adilman (Terry)

The tension mounts in Sunnyvale when Julian hears from J-Roc an[d] T that Cyrus is out of jail and he's got "fuckin' work to do"—work tha[t] involves a certain hash driveway, guns and revenge for several month[s] spent in jail. Ricky rushes Trinity out of the park while Julian tries t[o] enlist the help of J-Roc and T, who decline his request, sounding ver[y] Martin Luther King-like with all their talk of "peace" and "chillin' rathe[r] than killin'." A quick whistle and a few calls of "Here Cory and Trevo[r], Cory and Trevor, here boys!" later, and man's best friends arrive[,] tongues wagging, eager to help Julian by guarding the approach t[o] the park from Mrs. Peterson's roof.

"Mr. Lahey, the cock's done."

Bubbles pleads with Julian to find another way out of this mess. He['s] terrified and he's crying, and damn it, don't ya hate Cyrus for makin[g] Bubbles cry? Julian takes Bubs's words to heart and decides the[y] aren't going to settle this dispute with guns.

Cyrus and company arrive (dropped off at the park by Dennis an[d] Terry's grandmother) and note the "artwork" (a cowboy riding a cock[)] on Julian's old trailer. Julian confronts them with a white flag on [a] hockey stick and tells Cyrus a sweet-talking pack of lies, about ho[w] they all "look up to him" and that they're "sorry about stealing all th[e] hash, but you would have done it too"; he also emphasizes that it wa[s] Lahey who bailed them out of jail and who made the painting. Th[e] boys surrender the hash and Cyrus seems satisfied enough to leav[e] the park with Dennis and Terry. If only it were so simple. Moment[s] later, Cory misinterprets Julian's radio communication telling the[m] NOT to shoot and promptly opens fire. Cyrus and the brothers sho[ot] both Cory and Trevor in the arm for their trouble. A huge battle ensue[s] —the soundtrack is marginally quieter than *Apocalypse Now*—an[d] Julian, drink and gun in hand, collects the wounded Cory and Trevo[r] and throws them in the trunk for eventual transport to the hospital.

Just to add to the chaos, Ricky has a heart attack (remember thos[e] chest pains he's been having?) and dies—only to be resurrected b[y] Lahey's application of CPR, after Julian appeals to Jim's vanity. Th[e] cops arrive and next thing you know the boys—minus Bubbles—a[re] back in the joint.

rare photo

Trevor and Cory atop Mrs. Peterson's trailer, waiting to fuck up.

The boys hunker down behind the Shitmobile for cover. The Shitmobile is built like a tank, except for the rusty bits.

RICKYISMS

"The thing with me is that, I am smart. And I'm self-smarted, basically, by myself. Basically from nature and from smokin' drugs and doing different things I've self . . . self-learned myself. And that's the whole difference I guess, I don't need the books or the schools type things . . . I just get everything on my own—because of that, I'm alive right now. I mean, if I had read more books or tried to go into college or different things like that, I'd be dead right now because people say books and college are for to be ya to make you smarter, but they can also be for to be ya to get ya dead—which is what could have happened to me. My brain doesn't use enough oxygen because I don't have the whole thing filled with different stuff. And if it was full—it's only part full—that's why I'm alive right now. The guards in here are, 'Here, read this book and try to get smarter' and I'm like, I'll pretend to read it but I'm not going to really read it because my brain would be more full and I have another heart attack, I'm gonna die."

—No comment

 Just a flesh wound.

BAD BOYS SCALE

Lahey not quite drunk enough to be incapable of saving Ricky's life.

Julian almost returns Cyrus's hash, but Cory and Trevor fuck it up.

Ricky and Bubbles argue about who gets the "lateral cover fire" front-seat position versus the "centre cover fire" back-seat position. Bubbles gets ripped off again.

TRAILER PARK BOYS
Postcards from the Park

Trevor looks like he's stoned, drunk, wild-animal-attacked, shot or simply left in the trunk of a car, or all the above.

The hypnotic effect of bubbles on Bubbles is better than the best dope in town.

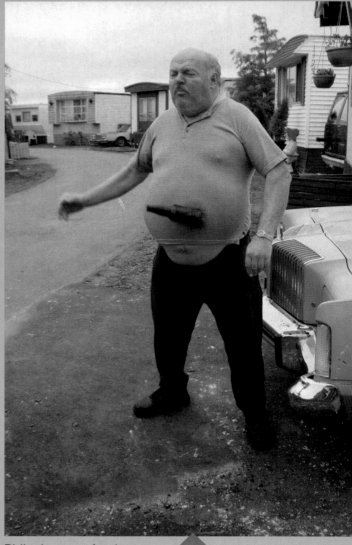

Phil takes one for the team.

Hotter than jalapeno.

Who says white guys in white pants can't dance.

SEASON 6

Ray, in the glory days before Randy evicts him to the dump.

nomesayin

MR. LAHEY'S SHIT ANALOGIES

"Better step off, Mr. Lahey."—Trevor telling Lahey to stop roughing him up
"Step off where, Trevor?"—Lahey
"A shit ledge."—Trevor

TRAILER PARK TIPS

Owning and operating a small retail operation is a perfect way to build the confidence and self-esteem absent in Cory and Trevor since conception. However, they need to understand a basic business concept: if a customer by the name of Ricky comes into your store (shed) and picks up two packs of smokes and then leaves without paying for them, eventually you will go out of business. This fundamental truth of Retail 101 is in no way related to the "law of supply and command," but it's true nonetheless.

In Cory and Trevor's store, there is a poster that reads "J-Roc Presents: Panty Hos."

Title: THE WAY OF THE ROAD
Air Date: APRIL 16, 2006

Writers: Mike Clattenburg, John Paul Tremblay, Robb Wells, Mike Smith, Jonathan Torrens, Iain MacLeod
Director: Mike Clattenburg
Guest Stars: James Swansburg (Officer Ted Johnston), Amy Kerr (Baby Mama #2), Valerie Fougere (Baby Mama #1)

As he eats yellowy brown goo (maybe Cheez Whiz, maybe rancid peanut butter?) out of a jar with a mini hockey stick, Ricky tells the camera that he's glad to be out of jail early this time, even if Julian has decided to stay a little longer. He and Ray have started a new business, picking up curbside recycling in the park, and life is looking pretty good. Even Lucy is taking him back, he thinks (she has a different opinion on this subject). Ray's pretty happy too, living in his old tractor trailer's sleeper cab, which is no longer connected to an actual truck. Doesn't bother him in the least. Bubbles is happiest of all: with Lahey too drunk to function and bother him, he can finally open up his long-dreamed of daycare centre for cats, Kittyland Love Center. Julian is still holed up in the joint (soon to be released), but things are pretty damn rosy in Sunnyvale.

"Ricky, don't tell anyone I'm living in the dump."

Alas, every silver cloud has a shitty lining, and in this case it's a wretchedly drunk Jim Lahey returning home in his New Yorker, its roof completely and utterly fuckin' gone. GONE! (How the car got this way proves to be one of the most puzzling mysteries of our time, on par with who shot JFK or the origins of crop circles.) Randy's had enough with the alcoholism so he breaks up with Lahey. Randy then wastes no time making a pitch to Barb for the top park job. The promotion to associate trailer park supervisor is his, she tells him, provided he can evict Ray. For some strange reason Barb is as horrified as Bubbles by the number of Ray's piss jugs littering the park.

Julian arrives home after a great time in jail; he made a killing in potato vodka sales, clearing $8,600. He buys a trailer from Barb (who eyes his biceps like a ravenous dog eyes a package of hot dog weiners) and tells her about his plans to get into real estate. The episode would have wrapped up very nicely except that Randy, on the premise of unpaid lot fees, actually succeeds in evicting Ray. Ray moves his sleeper cab home to the dump and vows not to return to Sunnyvale until Randy and Lahey are gone.

On a happier note, looks like J-Roc's getting some extra booties—baby booties, that is. Seems a couple of his ladies got J-Rocked up. Does this count as twins?

rare photo

The unveiling of Julian's new car spoiler—made from hockey sticks, of course.

Bubbles's excitement over the opening of Kittyland Love Center is dampened by the news that Ricky wants to start a junk business next door.

RICKYISM

"I got stung by one of those bumble cocksuckers again!"

—Ricky, complaining about wasps at the "recycles" pile

Bombus fervidus cocksuckerapidae
It's perfectly excusable that Ricky refers to the humble bumblebee as a "bumble cocksucker," given that the Latin name reads as follows: Bombus fervidus cocksuckerapidae. In fact, Ricky's confused—the insects swarming around the "recycles" pile are similar-looking yellow jacket wasps (Vespula cocksuckervespidae), looking for sugar and food scraps. Naturally, they're partial to pickled eggs and rum.

◄ Julian's potato vodka is selling like hot potatoes.

Title: THE CHEESEBURGER PICNIC
Air Date: APRIL 23, 2006

Writers: Mike Clattenburg, John Paul Tremblay, Robb Wells, Mike Smith, Jonathan Torrens, Iain MacLeod
Director: Mike Clattenburg
Guest Stars: Sam Tarasco (Sam Losco), Alvena Poole (Alvena), Bill Parsons (Bill), George Green (Officer George Green), James Swansburg (Officer Ted Johnston)

Come one, come all, it's the cheeseburger picnic—Randy's way of saying that law and order will reign supreme while he is park supervisor. Unhappy with Randy's ascendance, Lahey goes grovelling to Barb and tells her he might, just might, have a problem with booze. It's the boys' fault; so long as they're around, he won't be able to cope. He outlines his plan to pretend to be drinking hard again (after fourteen hours of sobriety) but secretly remain sober. If the boys see him wasted at the cheeseburger picnic, they'll let their "shit-guard" down. He'll be able to catch them red-handed at something illegal and send them back to jail.

"You probably heard that I was fired as supervale of the Sunnyparks park."

Meanwhile, Ricky and Julian are fighting over Cory and Trevor. The boys agree to split them up and Ricky initially wants Cory because he's smarter and Trevor's "dumb as fuck"; Bubs, however, points out that Trevor has "alien garbage-scooping arms" that would be perfect for hauling other people's property to the curb. (If it's at the curb, it's garbage, and therefore Ricky is not stealing it when he carts it away.) Ricky and Trevor head off to a well-to-do suburb and get to work not stealing. Mission accomplished, Ricky thoughtfully informs Trevor that the number 53 bus will get him right home and drives away.

With the picnic underway, Ricky and Ray start messing with Randy (revenge for Ray's eviction) by ordering up pizzas and plumbers, and sending them to Randy. To make matters worse ('cause it always gets worse), Lahey arrives, seemingly plastered out of his mind, crashing into tables, and announces to everyone that he doesn't give a shit what they do. When that greasy fuckin' caveman Sam Losco arrives with a work order to repave the park roads, Randy refuses to sign for it, which starts a fight, and Officer Ted Johnston arrests him. (Turns out, Ted explains with a twinkle in his eye, he was just helping Randy out of the jam by doing so.)

Ricky heads to Lucy's trailer and finds her dressed as a cop (assuming that an officer's cap, a police shirt knotted under the bra line, skin-tight silver hot pants and thigh-high white leather boots can comprise a police uniform) and Officer George Green handcuffed to the shower curtain rod wearing nothing but standard-issue police Fruit of the Looms. Ricky announces to Lucy that it is over between them. Meanwhile, across the park, Officer Ted gets Randy to wear a shirt. It seems some are taking it off while others are putting it on.

Mr. Lahey decides he doesn't need a glass for his beverage.

nomesayin

Towards the end of this episode a guy is playing with his expensive-looking remote-control car in front of Lucy's trailer when Ricky arrives in a rush in the Shitmobile. Remember the game rock, paper, scissors? Well, Shitmobile beats remote-control car.

TRAILER PARK TIPS

Ricky is trying his best to be a good dad and insists that Trinity file the serial numbers off her bicycle. Lots of fathers wouldn't go to the trouble. This kind of early guidance and TLC will pay off down the road when Trin hits her rebellious years and begins acting out by experimenting with alcohol and cigarettes. Wait, let's try that again . . . Trinity mastered booze and smokes by the time she was eight . . . and so Ricky's parenting skills are . . . never mind.

rare photo
Trevor's wait for the bus shouldn't be too long.

The long arm of the law will be reaching for some cheeseburgers as Sunnyvale gets used to life under the Randy regime.

RICKYISM

"Well, read these lips, Julian. I'm getting drunk as fuck, I'm doing drugs and I am going down to the cheeseburger picnic and I am fuckin' with Randy. Make my words."
—Ricky rejects the path of least resistance

The lawn furniture set is no match for Trevor's jaw and freakishly long arms.

BAD BOYS SCALE

Lahey's fake booze consumption. Ricky and Ray get hammered together.

Lucy is fuckin' baked.

Ricky uses Trevor to move lawn furniture to the curb so Ricky can then collect it as garbage. It's not stealing!

Grand opening of Garbageland, Ricky's used shit business.

nomesayin

Trevor is wearing a classic Rush *2112* T-shirt.

When Cory is thirsty, Julian pours his water into a dog bowl.

Steve Rodgers's Cable 10 business show is broadcast in high definition, and Bubbles comments, "It's high def, Ricky. Look how much clearer it looks." His set is about 11 inches wide and the picture resembles a blizzard, at dusk, seen through the Shitmobile windshield.

Ricky throws piss jugs onto Randy's trailer roof with the intensity and attention to form you would normally expect in the Olympic hammer throw.

Title: HIGH DEFINITION PISS JUGS
Air Date: APRIL 30, 2006

Writers: Mike Clattenburg, John Paul Tremblay, Robb Wells, Mike Smith, Jonathan Torrens, Iain MacLeod
Director: Mike Clattenburg
Guest Stars: Doug Barron (Steve Rodgers)

It's a regular entrepreneurial extravaganza in Sunnyvale. Just about everybody has a new business up and running. Ricky has opened Garbageland, Bubbles unveils Kittyland Love Center, Cory and Trevor have their variety store and Julian has opened a slightly less than legal building-supply centre. Cory and Trevor, and Bubbles through his own separate efforts, have convinced Steve Rodgers, host of Cable 10's business program, to visit the park and profile their new enterprises.

> ## "I wish Randy and Lahey would get back together, because this 'sexy' talk is starting to drive me nuts."

Lahey (still split from Randy) is continuing with his undercover surveillance of the boys, hoping to catch them in a criminal act; he is obviously content posing as the drunk bastard he always has been, stumbling around a "sexy, belligerent" Julian, watching for illicit activities. All the attention is creeping Julian out, but he continues to focus on his business anyway—oblivious to the sting Jim is dreaming up.

Across the park, Bubbles is working furiously to clean up around Kittyland, but it's one step forward, two steps back, because Ricky set up his garbage business right next door. Seems people actually throw out things that still have some value. Ricky's "discovered" this while accumulating his dubiously recycled products. The excess inventory has spawned Garbageland. Soon enough, Steve Rodgers, the "Live Eye of Local Business," arrives and begins interviewing the proprietors of CT Convenients Store. Cory and Trevor's revelation that the store sells individual cigarettes and pirated DVDs does little to endear them to Rodgers, and he soon moves on to check out Ricky and Bubbles's operations.

Ricky is showing off all his "used shit" on live television when he's attacked by bees (they're wasps, Ricky, wasps!). Then Lahey arrives, laden with piss jugs and seemingly drunk, looking to get a scrap going on live TV. Bubbles is devastated as the grappling begins and all of these assholes destroy his "expansive supervised play area for cats" in front of a TV audience. The sanity factor in the park is dropping faster than the barometer in the middle of a shiticane. Poor Bubbles—what will the kitties do now?

rare photo
It's a big fuckin' deal when Steve Rodgers and Cable 10 come to Sunnyvale.

Bubbles does his best to save his Cable 10 interview and Kittyland before total chaos ruins everything. Poor Bubbles.

RICKYISMS

"I think Bubbles should stop being so fuckin' selfnish and help me with Garbageland. The thing he doesn't understand is people who come for garbage and are going to buy garbage are going to have cats."
—Sounds like Bubbles has been trash talkin' Ricky's business

"Will you just promise me you'll use some sense of decorum on TV?"
—Bubbles to Ricky

"Bubbles, what are you worried about?
Of course I'll use demorcum on TV."
—Ricky

The CT Convenients Store is particularly convenient for the likes of Ricky, who never seems to pay for anything.

BAD BOYS SCALE

 Lahey pretending to be drunk for his undercover ops.

 No mention of dope.

 Julian is selling stolen construction material. Cory and Trevor are selling pirated DVDs and individual smokes.

Title: WHERE IN THE FUCK IS OSCAR GOLDMAN?
Air Date: MAY 7, 2006

Writers: Mike Clattenburg, John Paul Tremblay, Robb Wells, Mike Smith, Jonathan Torrens, Iain MacLeod
Director: Mike Clattenburg
Guest Stars: Pauline Kaill (Farm Lady), Corey Janes (Teacher), James Swansburg (Officer Ted Johnston)

Ricky's alarm clock rouses him from a deep sleep/stupor—no small task, given that he's sleeping in a discarded sewer pipe. He and Lucy have been worried about Trinity's school work of late, what with all the car drivin', bottle throwing and cigarette smokin'. Lucy has even consulted with Trin's teacher, whom she finds "attractive" (translation: she'd like to bang him).

The Cable 10 fiasco seems to have worked in Bubbles's favour, as his Kittyland daycare is thriving: "They must have just been able to see through the bullshit and know that I actually dole out love to the kitties." Unfortunately, Bubbles's care for Trinity's grade-six science project—a chicken named Oscar Goldman—is not quite so attentive. Bubs lets him go, for reasons he'd rather not talk about, and Ricky is going to be in deep shit with Lucy as a result: no chicken means Trinity flunks.

"What, you think you're the only guy to have his cock bit by a snake?"

Trevor suggests he and Ricky steal a chicken from a nearby farm; he recently saw one there that could be Oscar Goldman's "identical twin." Bubbles supports this plan: "Those shifty little bastards, they all look the same." They attempt to abduct Oscar's "twin," but a female farmer shows up and foils the plot by beating the snot out of Trevor. Ricky tries to explain that Trevor is an escaped mental patient and that he's a "mental doctor" who's come to collect Trevor in his "mental car." They barely escape.

Back at the park, Julian offers to pose as Trinity's dad—much to Lucy's delight—and to help her beg Trinity's teacher for an extension. Meanwhile Ricky seeks help from Ray at the dump. While Ricky's discussing the chicken problem over a pee, snakes collide and Ricky's is bitten. Soon much of Sunnyvale sets out in search of poultry and Ray tracks the scent right into Lahey's trailer. Ricky, thinking Jim is a thieving, dirty chicken rustler, trashes the place with such fury that Bubbles is scared into admitting, "It was me that let the dirty little fuckin' chicken out." Ricky apologizes to Lahey and generously offers Cory and Trevor to clean up as he bolts out the door with Oscar in hand.

Ricky rushes Oscar Goldman to the school and finds Julian and Lucy already pleading Trinity's case. Ricky convinces her teacher to accept the late science project, explaining, "You can't hold it against her just because her dad's stupid." That's real love.

The prospect of failing grade six due to a lost chicken doesn't sit well.

nomesayin

Check out Ricky's potato-chip breakfast: "0 Trans-fats." The HEALTHY kind!

Trinity's jean jacket has a Helix patch on the back.

rare photo
The only chicken Bubbles doesn't fear is wrapped in golden breading and shaped liked a finger.

Sarah consoles a dejected Trinity. Yet she has nothing to worry about: Ricky and Trevor are on the hunt for a new chicken.

RICKYISM

"That's a nice-looking chicken, right there. Just because her dad is a bit of a fuck-up—pardon my language in front of all these kids—doesn't mean she should fail grade six like her dad did."

—It's gonna take more than a blue-ribbon chicken to fix this mess

A chicken may or may not be tougher than Trevor, but the crazy chicken lady is, for damn sure.

BAD BOYS SCALE

Ray tracks Oscar Goldman for the free liquor and Ricky wakes up in a sewer pipe—had to be booze involved.

No sparkin' in this one.

Trevor's attempted theft of a chicken. (No animals were hurt in the production of this episode.)

Title: HALLOWEEN 1977
Air Date: MAY 14, 2006

Writers: Mike Clattenburg, John Paul Tremblay, Robb Wells, Mike Smith, Jonathan Torrens, Iain MacLeod
Director: Mike Clattenburg
Guest Stars: George Green (Officer George Green), James Swansburg (Officer Ted Johnston), Liam Cyr (Young Julian), Hans Petterson (Young Bubbles), Mitchell Taylor (Young Ricky), Bill Parsons (Bill), Alvena Poole (Alvena), Valerie Fougere (Baby Mama #1), Amy Kerr (Baby Mama #2)

Dr. J-Roc checks out his ladies and Randy. They all seem to be in their third trimester.

nomesayin

Things begin with Randy arriving, agitated and breathless, on Bubbles's doorstep. He explains to Bubs, in complete confidence, that he's confused about his sexuality: Sarah is really beginning to turn him on and he's worried that he might be . . . well, you know . . . straight. Bubbles invites him in to talk—and to cruise the Internet to find out what does it for Randy and what doesn't. A few clicks of the mouse later, Bubbles concludes that, in fact, most things do it for Randy.

"I got you this time, Julian, all on tape. You sexy prick."

Sarah figures that Randy is upset because he and Officer Ted Johnston have had a lovers' quarrel. If Ted's gift of an Abdominizer is any measure, he's not as captivated with Randy as Lahey was. Randy's also been staring at Sarah's boobs. Something's up, she suspects.

Thrilled to see Lahey boozing again and assuming Randy will be a pushover, Ricky continues his curbside theft business (unaware that Lahey is videotaping him). Randy might be leaving Ricky alone, but he does evict J-Roc, his two "baby mamas" and T. J-Roc tries reasoning with Randy and appeals to his belly, saying that he, of all people, should know what it's like to be expecting: "What? You ain't pregnant with a bucket of chicken?" J-Roc is soon on the street, along with a sweet old couple, Bill and Alvina, for failure to pay lot fees.

The opening shot of Randy sprinting to Bubbles's shed illustrates that this big man can actually move pretty quickly when he wants to. He may not be the great white hope of the world of track and field, but he sure looks to be the fastest guy in the park.

The Super-8 film of Halloween 1977 shows both Julian and Ricky dressed as drunk Chewbacca, and Bubbles as C-3PO (Ricky also seems to remember somebody being "Dark Vader.") There is also the odd KISS-attired rocker wannabe walking around in the background.

Sunnyvale is turning upside down and Randy is as confused as anyone. He even solicits advice from Sarah—between making passes at her—about the running of the park. Meanwhile, Lahey drops in on the boys and reveals he's actually been sober for the past month, and that he's been taping their criminal activities. Then he drops a bombshell: he's found an old Super-8 movie that documents Halloween night of 1977 in Sunnyvale. The grainy old film clearly shows that a prank pulled that night by Ricky and Julian on Officer Lahey directly resulted in JIM BEING THROWN OUT OF THE POLICE FORCE! He was never drunk on duty, as accused. In fact, according to Bubbles, Lahey was actually a pretty good guy back in the day. Bottom line: the blame for Jim Lahey's ruined career can be placed directly at the feet of Ricky and Julian (not surprisingly, Bubs did try to stop the prank). With this new evidence, Lahey manages to get a hearing with the Sunnyvale police force to make a case for his reinstatement.

MR. LAHEY'S SHIT ANALOGIES

"What's at work here is shit tectonics. When two shit plates strike, come together under incredible pressure, what happens, Bubbles? A shitquake."

rare photo
How a shirtless man stays undercover is anyone's guess.

Halloween 1977: Julian, Bubbles and Ricky out collecting candy, legally.

RICKYISMS

"J-Roc, I'm not a pezzamist, I'm an optometrist, but you have to keep your eye on Randy. He's fuckin' around, he's doing stuff."
—Do they make a cheeseburger Pez dispenser?

"If Randy thinks he's smartner than me, he's wrong."
—Who is the smartnest?

Glad to see J-Roc looking after his baby mamas and their babies with the "no-smoking" sign hanging from the rearview mirror.

BAD BOYS SCALE

	Lahey was not drunk when he was kicked off the force in 1977. A rare zero.
	Barely mentioned, really.
	The stunt the boys pulled on Lahey really screwed him over.

SEASON 6 EPISODE 6

Cory and Trevor actually DON'T fuck up. They create a great new weed trailer for Ricky.

nomesayin

Trevor has an FBI T-shirt on: "Female Body Inspector." Unfortunately, the only feminine form he has ever inspected intimately appeared to him exclusively in two dimensions.

TRAILER PARK TIPS

"If you want to quit the liquor, smoke weed. You can buy it off me."
—Ricky's addiction advice to Lahey (which might not be condoned by AA)

Title: GIMME MY FUCKIN' MONEY OR RANDY'S DEAD
Air Date: MAY 21, 2006

Writers: Mike Clattenburg, John Paul Tremblay, Robb Wells, Mike Smith, Jonathan Torrens, Iain MacLeod
Director: Mike Clattenburg
Guest Stars: Alvena Poole (Alvena), Bill Parsons (Bill), Richard Collins (Phil Collins), Sam Tarasco (Sam Losco), Amy Kerr (Baby Mama #2), Valerie Fougere (Baby Mama #1), George Green (Officer George Green), James Swansburg (Officer Ted Johnston), Maury Chaykin (Chief of Police)

When a garbage truck unloads all over his sleeper cab, Ray finds out the hard way that living in a garbage dump isn't as glamorous as people think. Ricky wants to get him out of there before he dies.

Jim Lahey has his own worries. Today he faces a police hearing to plead wrongful dismissal way back in 1977. He's nervous because Randy won't testify as a character witness, even after Lahey offers him forty-five hours of videotaped evidence against the boys. Desperate, Jim asks Bubbles to testify; in exchange, he promises not to fuck over the boys if he's reinstated (timely, because Julian is building a grow op trailer—with Cory and Trevor). Bubs agrees, but only with Lahey's promise in writing. By day's end, not only is Jim Lahey once again an officer of the law, but he has been accepted back by Barb.

"Flow with it. Go with the liquor, bud."

Bubbles tells the boys about his treaty with Lahey, and Julian presents Ricky with the finished grow-op. When Julian admits he couldn't have done it without Cory and Trevor, Ricky adds that the two of them are "pretty cool." Cory and Trevor almost burst into tears of joy.

This happy time can't last and the cops arrive to bust the boys. But true to his word, newly reinstated Officer Lahey busts up the bust; the boys are free to go. Sadly, while Barb is outside asking Randy to move in with them, Lahey's guzzling the booze. He's off the wagon and he's hit the ground friggin' hard—which is too bad, because that greasy bastard Sam Losco just abducted Randy at gunpoint. It seems Randy's complaints after the cheeseburger picnic cost Sam his paving job. Lahey enlists Ricky to help because he's the only guy with a mind "fucked-up enough" to help with such a fucked-up situation.

Lahey and Ricky meet Losco and a shootout ensues in which Ricky uses Phil Collins—a "human house"—as cover. They secure Randy's release when Ricky promises the greasy bastard a bag of weed. Miracle of miracles, Randy, Lahey and Ricky all drive back to the park together! Tranquility abounds. Lahey kicks booze, thanks to Ricky's advice to switch to weed; Ray drives around as assistant supervisor (a subclause of Bubs's agreement with Lahey); Julian has bought up all the evicted residents's trailers, renovated them and given them back no charge; Kittyland is booming; and Ricky's back with Lucy and Trinity, and says, "I don't know how life can get any better than this."

rare photo

Which will hold out longer?
Sam or Ricky's waistband?

Officer Jim Lahey reporting for duty.

"I've fuckin'
it with bees
tell you th
much. The
always aro
Ricky beca
he's soak
in liquor .
sugar on h
garbage ju
They're ju
attracted to
and I end
getting stur
the time. F
I hate bee
—Bubble

"Love yo
Julian.'
—Trevo

"Trevor, I k
you do. It'
known thi
but you de
have to be s
it all the ti
It's not co
Got it?"
—Julia

"Do you lo
though? Cor
the Trevst
—Trevo

"Yes, I do.
back to wo
—Julia

RICKY REVELATION

**"Actually, I had a really good
time getting drunk with ya."**
—Ricky to Lahey after they negotiate with
Sam Losco and successfully free Randy

In the history of human
shields, few carry more
weight than Phil Collins.

BAD BOYS SCAL

Lahey on the booze, the
off the booze, then on th
booze. . .

Lahey never on the dope
but, then, on the dope-HA

Randy's abduction is pretty hardcore, b
no one goes to jail. Subtract two bullets

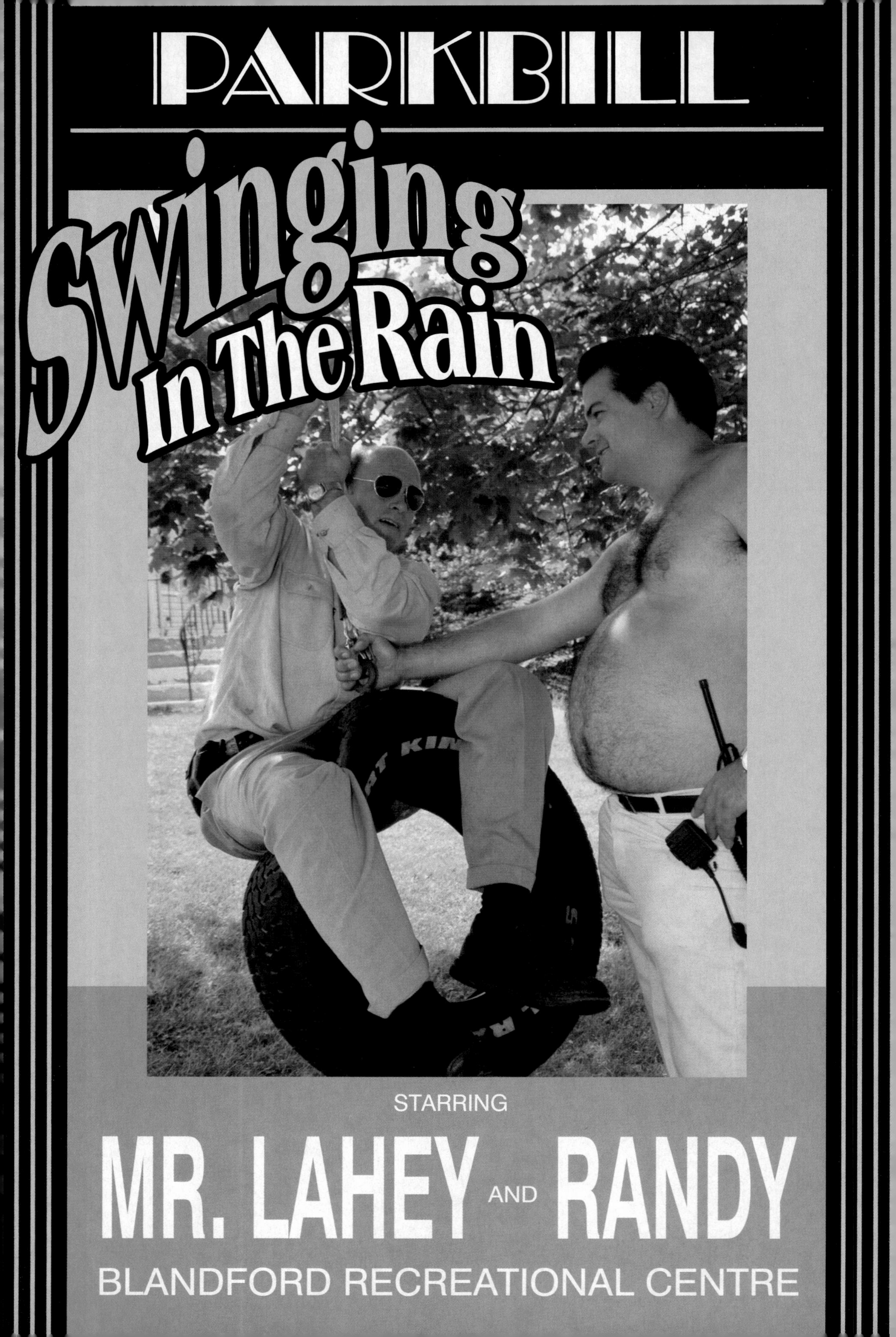
PARKBILL
Swinging In The Rain
STARRING
MR. LAHEY AND RANDY
BLANDFORD RECREATIONAL CENTRE

OTHER SHIT

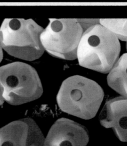

The Wrong Stuff

Word was the project was dangerous, but the response back from Commander Bubbles was unequivocal: "Count me in." The search began for a new breed of men in Sunnyvale—men who were fearless. Ambitious, brave, dedicated, gutsy men. Some with more gut than others.

Soon Commander Bubbles would be joined in his quest for semi-intelligent life by the handsome and supremely confident Julian, a born leader who was thankful he grew up in a trailer park that had always brought his best to the fore. The enterprise solidified its ranks with its third and final member—a brash, young Shitmobile jock capable of only two speeds: flat out or incarcerated. This risk-taking, cocky son of a bitch was not only intrepid, but also completely ignorant of what the word "intrepid" meant. To the public at large, he answered to the name Ricky. But within the closed brotherhood of the space program, where loyalty and guts were the only qualities that mattered, he had one name and one name only: Ricky.

The trio reveled in the adoration of their public (Treen and Trinity), but behind the heroic image they were flesh-and-blood-and-alcohol young men with real fears (ma cops), frustrations (Lucy) and conflicts ("Fuck off, Lahey!"

> **"We got a complaint that people are getting drunk and high and playing space in the middle of the street."**—*Randy*
>
> **"Yeah. Us"**—*Ricky*

This is the story of the very special few at the very top of their game—the elite fraternity of men who would go t any lengths to acquire, build and fire a "fully function rocket kit" into the upper limits of Sunnyvale's hazy uppe atmosphere. Did the boys have what it takes for th mission? You bet they did, pal. They had plenty. The had: The Wrong Stuff.

Great Space Quotes in History

"That's one small step for a man, one giant leap for mankind."
—Neil Armstrong

"DECENT!"
—Commander Bubbles

"Breaker, breaker, come in Earth, this is Rocket Ship 27. Aliens fucked over the carbonator number four and I'm going to try and refuckulate it and land on Juniper. Hopefully they got some space weed. Over."
—Ricky

"Naysa, power rockets are firing all over the place. They got lasers and they're shooting and . . . Ah, Bubbles, I can't fuckin' do this!"
—Ricky

"I'm going to get my spacesuit, boys, and we're going to get this dirty cocksucker in the air."
—Commander Bubbles

167

Gun Safety?

Gun safety is no laughing matter. Well, actually . . . it is. The way we see it, our boys handle weapons with at least as much concern for the safety of their fellow citizens as do the folks pursued in your typical episode of *Cops*. Still, there's always room for improvement when it comes to using or storing a firearm; always follow these basic Sunnyvale gun safety rules and odds are Ricky might not get shot.

- Know your target (could be a Christmas tree salesman, barking dog or squirrel) and what's behind it. If you don't know both or either, remember the cardinal rule: shoot first and think second.

- Know how to use the gun safely. Make sure there is always ammunition in the magazine and a bullet in the chamber. Remember, a gun's safety device isn't foolproof, so you might as well leave it off.

- When shooting at irritating, weed-killing squirrels, always do so in a rodent-induced rage. And remember to put the correct squirrel-killing ammunition in your automatic.

- If your name is Cyrus, make sure you openly brag about the safety always being off just as you stuff a giant gun down the front of your pants.

- Store guns so they are not accessible to unauthorized persons. Unauthorized persons usually include eight-year-old girls named Trinity.

- Never combine alcohol, over-the-counter prescriptions an[d] other drugs while you are waving a loaded .357 Magnu[m] around in a crazy fashion. If you can't help yourself, and th[e] urge to kill Ricky is powerful, at least leave the smashin[g] floral-print dress, as well as the elegant dynamite wrap, [at] home. Kinda gives "dressed to kill" a whole new meanin[g.]

- If Ricky gets shot, keep in mind that he'll quite likely g[et] shot again, so stay clear for a while.

- Be really careful around potato guns! The muzzle veloci[ty] approaches 60 metres per second and if you get tagge[d] (Ricky, are you listening?) with Bud the Spud, it's gonn[a] fuckin' hurt.

- Remember to call a halt to the shooting if, in the middle of [a] gun battle, somebody gets hurt.

Trailer & Track

SUPER CART SHOOT OUT!

EXCLUSIVE!

NEW SHITMOBILE UNVEILED

	2006 BM▓▓ ▓oadster	Bubbles's Go-Kart
Current list price	Would buy a lot of pepperoni	Ask Ricky
Engine	dohc 3.2-liter	A real beauty—cocksucker's red
Horsepower	330 bhp @ 7900 rpm	Enough to haul Ricky
Torque	260 lb-ft @ 4900 rpm	Cocksucker's got plenty
Transmission	6-speed manual	Behind the seat
0-100kph	4.9 sec	Almost as fast as a weed-free Steve French
Braking 0-100kph	35 meters	Don't know—but there will be dust. Lots of dust.
Lateral acceleration	0.89g	Huh?
Speed thru 213m slalom	109kph	Huh? Again
Fuel economy	Cory and Trevor need to siphon plenty to run this cocksucker	Cory and Trevor's health won't be damaged too much to keep this bastard going
Length	408 cm	Fits in the shitmobile
Width	177cm	Still fits in shitmobile
Height	129 cm	Fits under a trailer
Wheelbase	248 cm	Don't know what this is
Ricky Towing Capacity	Friggin' awful	Friggin' awesome!
Curb weight	1483 kilos	No curbs in Sunnyvale

KARTWHEELS

We all know the coolest ride in Sunnyvale, hands down, is Bubbles's go-kart. Muscular styling, a decent red engine, combined with nimble and balanced handling, make this a vehicle coveted by any *Trailer Park Boys* fan.

Compared with the Shitmobile, Bubbles's kart feels tight and responsive while cornering; its attitude is noticeably flatter and not as friggin' pitch sensitive as, say, Cyrus's red Corvette. The go-kart's precise steering gives Bubbles the confidence to simply drive it as if he were riding a rail: dial in the steering, and this cocksucker will get you there with a minimum of trailing throttle oversteer. As an added bonus, the front end obeys directional inputs as unquestioningly as Cory and Trevor do. There's no hesitation and little is lost in translation between driver, car and road surface—particularly when towing a heavy load of shopping carts.

On both Sunnyvale roads and at the mall, the go-kart responds to its driver with a pleasing level of calm predictability—even while burning past Lahey's New Yorker at full throttle. Approaching top speed, the kart's front end edges out before its tail, but not so much that you think the cocksucker is going to pile into Ray's wheelchair, which is, no doubt, weaving drunkenly all over the lane. We should also point out that the brakes perform nicely on park streets, slowing the kart with such confidence Bubbles never worries about skidding into Trinity while she's having a smoke break on the edge of the playground.

The one-cylinder Briggs & Stratton motor smoothly delivers a whopping 7.5 horses right up to the red line. The result? Plenty of torque to haul a frequently intoxicated Ricky around the park.

All in all, our road test of this baby was fuckin' beautiful. It doesn't have a hockey-stick spoiler, a fancy siren on the dash or a roomy interior like the Shitmobile, but this much we do know: if the imports want to compete with this cocksucker, they've got their fuckin' work cut out for them.

Towing capacity for Bubbles's go-kart is fuckin' decent. Pulling carts and Ricky is an effortless chore for this workhorse.

HOLY SHIT!

It's remarkably below expectation and excitingly unoriginal

esus Christ, boys! Talk about a tough ssignment—road testing of one of the most remarkable cars to ever grace the ighways and byways of Sunnyvale railer Park. In 2007, the 1975 Chrysler hitmobile delivers the non-upgrades ou'd expect, plus bolder non-styling, l-new non-hybrid fuelling and an all-o-familiar dash, nonsporty handling nd increased unreliability.

ttle effort has gone into redefining the hitmobile's style, aimed at attracting new, slightly less stoned Ricky, while ll appealing to a Ricky who is merely runk. To this end, the exterior design oks exactly like the car it hasn't placed. Not gone is the rusty, green-nd-black, piece-of-shit look; nor is it placed by a more interesting or, dare e say, muscular build. Compared with st year's car, the new Shitmobile omes across as a substantial piece of it, rather than just an adequate, urposeful piece of shit.

ut on to the question most asked in utomotive circles: what's under the ood? Is this vehicle all about tempting on-styling and rollered-on black paint, does the story get more exciting? es and no. Powertrain choices remain nchanged from last year: the standard

engine—a non-reworked version of Chrysler's thundering 5,000 cubic inch V8—produces less horsepower than it did a year ago and battles the road like any thirty-two-year-old motor, serving up shit performance and gas mileage that makes Saudi Arabians weep with joy. Transmission options remain non-optional—"Drive doesn't work but neutral does. Neutral is park and reverse is second. If you want to use reverse, put it in drive."

We'd also like to welcome the 2007/ 1975 Shitmobile Hybrid. This is a completely separate, non-existent model that features Chrysler's not-patented Hybrid Weed-Fuelled Drive to pair the 5,000 cubic inch engine up to an electric motor. This more eco-friendly Shitmobile distinguishes itself from the rest of the lineup by simply not existing.

The all-new 2007/1975 Shitmobile has big shitty shoes to fill, which is one thing it does with ease. Expect pricing to be right around the "free" mark, with the current model starting at just less than the price of a bucket of Jiffy Wine.

The interior is pre-filthed and tumbled like prewashed jeans in a giant rock-filled washer.

Optional sleeping door is exclusive to the Shitmobile. Faux fur pillow not included.

LET'S EAT!

Sunnyvale's Top Ten Favourite Foods

1. Cheeseburgers
2. Chicken fingers
3. Pepperoni
4. Julapanoh chips
5. Fried bologna
6. Pickled eggs
7. Zesty Mordant chips
8. Weed brownies
9. Licorice
10. Canned ravioli

Honorable Mentions

Steve French weedjitas
Sam's greasy hot dogs
Trailer-burnin' french fries
Randy's Viagra burgers
Mr. Lahey's blue jay burger

Bubbles's "Delicious Things" Pickled Eggs

- Put lots of eggs in a big jar (the more eggs the better).
- Add 1 cup water.
- Add ½ cup vinegar.
- Add 1 tsp sugar.
- Add a ton of fuckin' salt.
- Add a bay leaf if you're some friggin' gourmet chef.
- Garnish with weed.
- Pickle the bastard for two days.

This dinner-party delight can be made ahead of time and served cold, preparing you should guests drop in unexpectedly. We suggest serving with a light rum or any other alcoholic substance readily at hand.

Per serving
Calories: Oh yeah.
Protein: Sure.
Total fat: Okay.
Dietary fibre: Maybe.
Sodium: Yup.

Ricky's Peanut Butter Summer Surprise

Nothing says summer quite like a quick and easy meal served up in the great outdoors. Some peanuts, a little tobacco and a hefty tumbler of rum is all it takes.

- Open a jar of peanut butter and serve with a mini hockey stick
- Cut the top six inches off a two-litre plastic pop bottle and pou your rum into the remainder (serve lukewarm).
- Light up a smoke and take drags between mouthfuls of peanut butter and swigs of rum. Deeelicious!

Per serving
Calories: Do Ricky and Julian go to jail much?
Protein: Sure, why not?
Total fat: Yup.
Dietary fibre: Do cigarettes have fibre in them? If so, then fine.
Sodium: In peanut butter? Fuck off! No way.

Microwaveable Submarine Sandwiches

Best served between 1:00 and 3:00 a.m., these crowd pleasers never disappoint after a night of rum and weed.

- Hop in Shitmobile and drive to all-night convenience store.
- Put sub in microwave for at least forty-five seconds and no more than one minute (any longer and the lettuce will liquify).
- Eat it on the spot.

Per serving
Calories: Geez, ya gotta think so!
Protein: Sometimes.
Total fat: The package says it isn't too bad.
Dietary fibre: The package has more fibre than the sub.
Sodium: Yup again. Lots of grams or ounces or something used to measure little things.

Ricky Passed Out

Dope Growing

Bogus Theater
Rehearsals

Mr. Lahey's
Surveillance
Stake-Outs

Sometimes you can't find a toilet when you really need one.

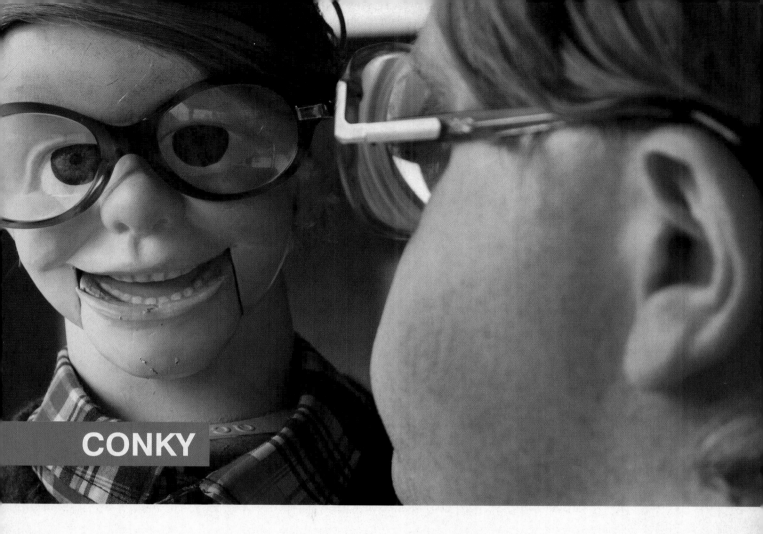

CONKY

He Can't Be All Bad . . .

Confrontational, undiplomatic, insensitive—alright, he's a downright nasty little fucker; but Conky must have some redeeming features, right? After all, he's tight with Bubbles, and to paraphrase an old saying or two, any friend of Bubbles's is indeed a friend of mine. Admittedly, it's not easy finding good things to say about an imperious puppet that makes even casual acquaintances wonder if a crack squad of Maryland exorcists shouldn't pack up their collars and holy water and catch the next high-speed ferry to Nova Scotia. But he can't be all bad, can he?

Conky is kind of cute. Under different circumstances he might have had a career in children's television (provided all the other puppets—and puppeteers, soundmen, cameramen, lighting guys, gaffers and voice-over actors —were given strict instructions to never turn their backs on him). He'd probably need a better nickname than "Little Fuckface" though.

He already seems to be a natural for the musical parts of a kids' show. His talent for conveying the heart wrenching strains of early-sixties ballads is so righteous . . . Brother.

Conky opens up a fresh line of communication between Bubbles and the boys. If Bubs is feeling frustration or anger about Ricky's latest fuckup, Conky comes right to the point, suggesting that Ricky consider a "brain transplant."

Like a happy-go-lucky canine—or Cory and Trevor— Conky makes for pleasant company in the car, yowling his delight out the window at the passing countryside. His responding to the normally rhetorical question "Who's a good boy? Who's a good boy?" with "I'm a good boy, Bubbles," was a little creepy, though.

He is endearingly loyal and will gladly defend Bubbles with a poisonous barb aimed straight at Ricky's self-esteem—so long as Bubbles understands that the master-and-puppet relationship is somewhat unorthodox in their case: "You just remember, I call the shots around here, Bubbles. You got it?" "Yes, Conky." "Good."

Someone could really use a smoke or a drink or a pickled egg.

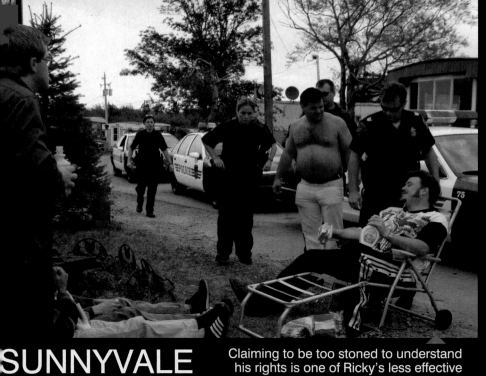

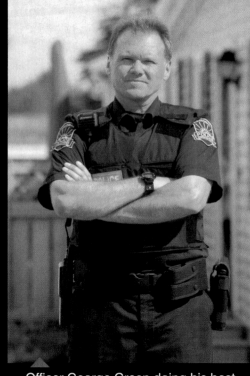

SUNNYVALE
COPS

"...little thing called evidence."

Claiming to be too stoned to understand his rights is one of Ricky's less effective arrest-prevention strategies.

Officer George Green doing his best to keep Sunnyvale prisons empty.

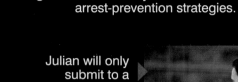

Julian will only submit to a one-armed handcuff. It's udder chaos.

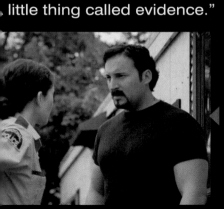

Officer Erica Miller. Putting her job ahead of Julian was a hard decision, a very hard decision.

Ricky's hair is too big to be arrested.

Officer Ted Johnston, made Randy wear a shirt. Does he have some sort of magical cop powers?

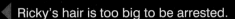

The cows are suspiciously oblivious to the police helicopter overhead.

Ricky may not appear to be a lawyer, but Bubbles sure looks like an eyewitness.

SUNNYVALE'S BEST Gun BATTLES

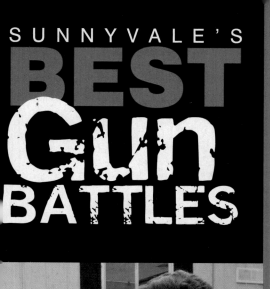

1. Season 1, Episode 2: "Fuck Community College, Let's Get Drunk and Eat Chicken Fingers" Ricky has an ongoing gun battle with a barking neighbourhood dog. (It's not a fair fight because Ricky's drunk and his aim is off.)

2. Season 1, Episode 4: "Mrs. Peterson's Dog Gets Fucked Up" Ricky gets shot by Trinity and a stranger with a shotgun in the same day.

3. Season 1, Episode 6: "Who the Hell Invited These Idiots to My Wedding?" The grocery-store robbery the night before Ricky and Lucy's wedding includes one of the most spectacular of all the spectacular gunfights in Sunnyvale history. Ricky, Julian, Bubbles and Cory and Trevor fire 231,009 rounds of ammunition at Ricky, Julian, Bubbles and Cory and Trevor.

4. Season 2, Episode 5: "The Bible Pimp" The boys get into a huge gunfight with stripper Tanya and her bible pimp, Hampton. Fortunately Tanya's figure was not damaged by gunfire.

5. Season 2, Episode 7: "The Bare Pimp Project" A huge gunfight with Cyrus, the greasy bastard Sam Losco and the cops. Ends with the Airstream trailer flipping over.

6. Season 3, Episode 1: "Kiss of Freedom" Ricky gets into a gun battle with Julian's ice-cream carts.

7. Season 5, Episode 10: "The Shit Blizzard" Thanks to a Cory and Trevor fuck-up, enough shots are fired to put this battle on the cover of *Guns & Ammo* magazine.

CYRUS'S

TOUGH TALK

Tough guys. Bronson, Eastwood, the Green Bastard. Guys who get premium performance from their rides even though they fill them with regular gas. Guys so tough that when they order fries from a drive-thru, they get super-size without asking. Some are born tough and some are made tough by life's cruel turns of fate, while others dream they can be tough by simply reading or watching TV and imitating those guys. Well this interview is for you dreamers out there. Following are some choice bits of tough meat to chew on from Sunnyvale's exiled tough guy, Cyrus.

Hello Cyrus, thanks for taking the time to talk to us.
Fuck off, I got work to do.

We're here for the tough-guy interview . . . Remember?
Well, you can fuck off later then.

Fair enough. Let's get to it. What does the word "tough" mean to you?
Means I can tell you or anyone else to fuck off whenever I want.

So if I told you to fuck off, that would make me tough?
No, because I wouldn't fuck off. You're tough if you tell someone to fuck off and they fuck off. If they don't fuck off, you're not tough.

So what do you do when you tell someone to fuck off and they don't?
Oh they fuck off, and if they don't fuck off, my little friend here [lifts his shirt to reveal a pistol] makes them fuck off.

So does that mean you're tough because you have a gun?
No, it means I'm tough and have a gun . . . so fuck off.

Okay, what about the whole "tough" look? Do you wear the black leather jacket to look more tough?
Are you fucking serious? I already told you, I'm tough. I don't need a leather jacket to tell you to fuck off.

But doesn't telling me to fuck off while wearing the jacket seem more tough than if you, say, told me to fuck off and you were wearing a sweater?
Why the fuck would I be wearing a sweater?

Well, you said you're tough and wearing the leather jacket has nothing to do with it, so I figured you would be just as tough wearing a sweater.
What colour is the sweater?

Does it matter? What colour do you like?
Black is good.

Okay. A black cotton sweater. Would you be tough in that?
Make it a leather sweater. A black leather sweater. Now, fuck off.

I see you drive a red Corvette. You know, just like that Prince song, "Little Red Corvette." Are you a fan?
Am I a what?

A fan. Of Prince? He wears leather, although I think it's purple.
What the fuck are you talking about?

Sorry. Your car, is it another part of being tough? And I say that with the complete understanding that you are already tough without the gun, leather or car.
The ladies like the car.

So are women attracted to you because of the car or because you're tough? Women like tough guys, don't they?
You're fucking weird . . . I think you better fuck off.

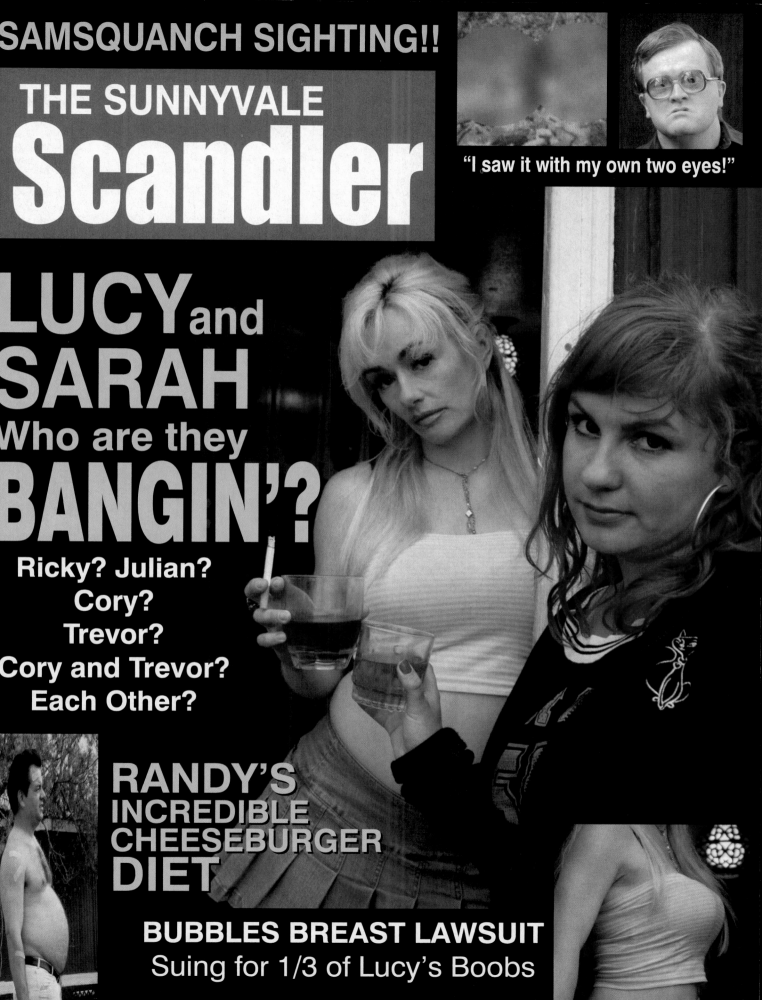

SAMSQUANCH SIGHTING!!

THE SUNNYVALE
Scandler

"I saw it with my own two eyes!"

LUCY and SARAH
Who are they
BANGIN'?

Ricky? Julian?
Cory?
Trevor?
Cory and Trevor?
Each Other?

RANDY'S INCREDIBLE CHEESEBURGER DIET

BUBBLES BREAST LAWSUIT
Suing for 1/3 of Lucy's Boobs

TAKE COVER! BOTTLE KIDS ATTACK!

Dear Trailer Park Advisors,

My friends at my online Lord of the Rings *gaming club and I were wondering: who would win in a battle between the Orcs of Mordor and the Bottle Kids of Sunnyvale?*

Yours,
Hypothetically Curious

Dear Hypothetically Curious,

First of all, we'd like to congratulate you for taking time out of your busy schedule of full-blown geekdom to ask what may well be the stupidest question we have ever entertained. Well done. Having said this, we'd like to respond with another question: why don't you ask your girlfriend if she has the answer?

Although these Orc thingies you make reference to are clearly big, muscly, greasy bastards with serious anger-management issues, it's not like they're any tougher than the boys (or Randy for that matter—pants off, of course), and the Bottle Kids never back down from those guys. In addition to the youngsters' complete lack of fear, and elevated blood-sugar levels, they hurl liquor bottles at very high velocities, while maintaining a punishing-bowel-loosening-rate of fire. In light of this, any numerical advantage Dark Lord Sauron Whatshisname might have with his rampaging army of Orcs just doesn't seem all that impressive. And we haven't even mentioned the Green Bastard's participation should things get a little rough for our side . . .

We hope this helps.
TPA

WHAT IF

everyone at Sunnyvale went to the same optometrist as Bubbles?

Sunset at Sunnyvale.

Acknowledgements

d like to begin by thanking everyone involved in the creation and production of this extraordinary television eries. In particular, thanks to Barrie Dunn and Michael olpe for their wonderful hospitality when we visited lalifax in 2006; thanks to Mike Clattenburg for allowing us b be extras in season seven (I hope you'll agree my uanced consumption of the ~~Tim Horton's~~ doughnut was method acting at its best); thanks to John Paul Tremblay, obb Wells and Mike Smith for allowing themselves to be hotographed for the trillionth time with a couple of star-truck fans; and thanks to Mike Tompkins and Scott Munn or providing the treasure chest of amazing photos from e set.

would like to say thank you to Brad Martin and Duncan hields at Random House for supporting the project, and nany thanks to their excellent sales group—Trish, Roni, teve, Mike R. (glad you dig the show), Tim, Maylin, Mike F. glad you dig the show) Marlene, Don (glad you dig the how), Cheryl and David—for selling Can Lit of an entirely ifferent order. Thanks to Tracey (glad you dig the show) nd her marketing team and Lisa's online group. I'm articularly grateful to our publicist, Cathy Paine, for her xpertise, humour and energy in promoting this book.

o our publisher, Anne Collins, I extend heartfelt gratitude or understanding that my interpretation of Martin Luther ing, Jr.'s immortal words, "I have a dream," means writing

a book about the *Trailer Park Boys*. (It's no coincidence that the great man's image appears on one of Ricky's shirts.) Thanks again for everything! To Michelle MacAleese, your encouraging words and *Trailer Park Boys* "expertise" were quite welcome. And last, but certainly not least, a huge round of applause for our editor, Craig Pyette. Your editorial knowledge (and humour) have been a gift from above; but if you tell me to shorten this acknowledgments page, I'm gonna tell you to frig off! You've been great.

To all of you at Random House I extend the following wise words: one cannot survive on promoting Shakespeare alone.

I have to acknowledge my friend Mark Pagliacci. Your excellent sense of humour picked up on this show early and you made me watch. To my great friend, co-conspirator and spiritual advisor, Don Wininger, I say excellent work. (Maybe we should re-form Eleven and tour Japan?)

Finally, I want to thank my family, my wife, Jan, and my children, Anna and Maddie, for all your support. I know it's not been easy being a Trailer Park widow and orphans for the last ten months. I love you guys!

—Matthew Sibiga

et me start by echoing all the thanks that Matthew stated bove. The opportunity to work with the creation that is railer Park Boys has been wonderful in many ways. But s I finish these last few lines, I could really use a rum and epperoni stick. In fact, I may get drunk as fuck. Meeting arrie Dunn, Mike Volpe and the cast was "very cool," ccording to my kids. I agree. Special thanks to Blain lorris for writing such a great theme song for the show. hat's what hooked me first. The first time I watched the railer Park Boys with my teenage son, was the licrophone Assassin episode. You Remember—when Roc gets caught "pulling his goalie." Nothing like overt nasturbation to get the dialogue going between father nd son. But that's what I love about the *Trailer Park Boys*. ne show treats life's more interesting moments with umour and a disarming context that allows viewers to ke themselves a little less seriously.

veryone at Random House have been a joy to work with, particular, our editor Craig Pyette—thanks, Craig nother em dash for you). Also, thanks to Pam Robertson nd James Grainger for their keen editing eyes and to the

Random House art department for tolerating a PC user. Thanks to Chadrick Rode for assisting with file production.

I'd like to thank all my friends and family who generously listened to my book tales. And for your encouragement, my sincere appreciation.

Matthew Sibiga and I were roommates our first year at university. Since then, we have survived five weeks in Europe; argued over English football; teamed up to beat the crap out of our buddy Rob, whom we still miss; been in a Spinal Tap tribute band; and written a book about one of our favourite TV shows. Can't wait to see what's next. Thanks, Matt, for your friendship and making this possible.

Finally, my greatest joy in life is my wife, Trish, and children, James and Lauren. They helped with research on the book and continual support. Now that the book is complete, I'm looking forward to spending more time with them and a bit less with Ricky, Julian and Bubbles.

—Don Wininger

Bubbles has left the park.